Here's another one I made earlier...

Scripture Union
craft resources for
3s to 11s

Compiled by
Christine Orme

Scripture Union
207–209 Queensway,
Bletchley, MK2 2EB,
England

© Scripture Union 2000

With grateful thanks

to all the writers who have contributed to SALT 3 to 4+, SALT 5 to 7+ and SALT 8 to 10+ between the years 1995 – 1998. Without their hard work and creativity, this book could not have been produced.

ISBN 978 1 85999 338 5

British Library Cataloguing-in-Publication Data

A catalogue record for this book is available from the British Library.

Cover design: Tony Cantale Graphics

Internal design: Tony Cantale Graphics

Illustrations: Anna Carpenter, Angela Edwards

Page layout by Creative Pages
www.creativepages.co.uk

Desk editor: Sarah Mayers

Printed and bound in Great Britain by
Marston Book Services Limited, Didcot

Contents

Foreword

WHEN my children were small we had a big box at the bottom of the stairs, known as the 'moggle' box if you were under five! Into it went pots and packaging of every kind. Nothing was wasted! With the aid of scissors, glue and powder paint (Early Learning Centre had just opened its first shops!) household junk was recycled into weird and wonderful creations. I think my girls had as much fun from that box as from the rest of their toys put together.

As they grew up I had to find less interesting, if more conventional, ways of disposing of packaging, but I always kept handy a box containing basic craft materials, aware that the contents were guaranteed to occupy any young visitor aged two to ten. Now my eldest daughter teaches infants so I'm collecting cereal packets and cardboard tubes again, knowing that they will be used creatively. For we are creative beings, made in the image of a Creator God and that creativity is very evident in young children, who are the most enthusiastic 'makers' you could ever hope to meet.

A generation ago teachers in training had impressed on them this ancient saying: 'I hear and I forget; I see and I remember; I do and I understand'. It summarised the new 'child-centred' approach to teaching, which in turn affected the way we work with children out of school. Craft activities are an essential part of the learning process. The child who does or makes something in connection with what she is learning is far more likely to remember than the one who sits passively (or disrupts because he is bored) – and 'making things' has never been more exciting than it is today. In addition to those cereal packets and yoghurt pots which are still the mainstays of much 'making', it is easy to find many wonderful materials and simple-to-use resources once available only to professionals. Many of us have access to photocopiers or scanners, so reproducing templates has never been simpler, and getting spectacular results is within the grasp of even the most ham-fisted, amongst whom I count myself.

I wonder why you picked up this book? Perhaps you used its predecessor, *Here's One I Made Earlier* and need more ideas for things to do with a lively group of children. Maybe, like me, you have ideas but find it difficult to work them out because you're not particularly artistic. Perhaps you want an all-age activity for the next family service, or someone has given you 1000 paper plates (these things happen!) and you are looking for creative ways to use them...

Whatever the reason, if you have access to scissors, glue and a few other bits and pieces, this book is for you. I hope you enjoy using it as much as I enjoyed compiling it – and here I must thank my youngest daughter, Stephanie, who sacrificed her half-term holiday to test all the recipes, check text and illustrations, and sort out the computer when it had me baffled, and Helen, my second daughter, who helped me put everything together again after the first manuscript got lost in the post!

Christine Orme

Introduction

When compiling a resource book of this kind it's always difficult to know how much general information of the 'what you need' and 'how to make' kind to include.

There are, however, a few golden rules for making things with children:

1 The first (as the titles of both books in this series suggest) is ALWAYS TRY THINGS OUT AT HOME, in good time beforehand. That way, you will spot potentially tricky bits, or maybe find easier ways of doing something. You will also be able to work out how much you need to do beforehand if your children are young, or if you don't have much time or extra adult help.

2 The second rule (even if you are usually very 'laid-back'), is ORGANISE YOUR ROOM AND EQUIPMENT BEFORE YOU START. Even four children falling in delight on piles of paper, glue, scissors and so on, can seem like forty if you don't know what you – or they – are doing! Make sure you have everything you need organised and laid out beforehand in the order in which you are going to need it for the activity. Make sure too that you have enough adult helpers, especially for fiddly or complicated things –children quickly get bored and will find other very creative things to do with the glue if there is a queue of ten others ahead of them, all waiting for your help with one awkward bit!

3 Thirdly, make sure you show and explain to your group exactly what they are going to do BEFORE they are allowed anywhere near the materials! Make this a firm rule every time you do craft activities, and the children will accept it and listen to instructions. This should prevent them doing things in the wrong order or cutting along that line they were meant only to fold...

4 Finally, DON'T BE OVER-AMBITIOUS. A craft activity doesn't have to be complex to be satisfying: some of the best ideas are very simple. Young children are more interested in the process than the product – it's the actual *doing* that they enjoy, rather than the result – a fact which may partly account for the number of things which get left behind after the session.

Many activities use 'junk' or scraps, and that's fine. Most churches have tight budgets, especially for children's activities! Sometimes however, you need to provide good quality materials, for example if children are to make a card to take home or for a special occasion. It's easy to think, 'Oh – they can use computer paper.' But we need to consider what unspoken message we're communicating to children by the materials we offer them to use. A good test is to ask ourselves, 'If I were to do this activity with the adults, would I offer them the same materials to use as those I'm offering to the children?'

In the same vein, what are we communicating to children about their value

HOW TO USE THIS BOOK

Here's One I Made Earlier was divided into sections according to the type of activity (puppets, pictures, models, etc) and gave very detailed instructions for making almost anything! This book contains lots more useful ideas and is arranged differently. The sections deal with various themes such as **Bible people** or **God's world** and in each section you will find different craft activities linked to that theme, sometimes with cross-referencing to another section. So if you are about to consider Noah, for instance, you could look in **Bible people** and find there detailed instructions for specific 'Noah' activities, with a cross reference to rainbow activities in another section, and doves and ravens in others. If you're not sure where to start, use the index.

In addition there is a short section called **Multi-use resources** which give some ideas for craft activities which can be used with almost any topic, and at the back you will find pages of templates. Recipes for clay and playdough (used in a number of activities) are given on these pages.

Home-made baking clay

(enough for four squares or rectangles)
You will need:
   4 cups plain flour
   1.5 cups hot water
   1 cup salt.
Mix the salt into the hot water before adding the flour. Mix to a soft dough. Form into individual squares or rectangles and place on a baking sheet or tray before the activity commences. Bake in a slow oven at 300°F/ Gas Mark 2, for 2 hours or until hard. Increase quantities proportionately for a larger group.

This clay is useful for models and for badges which you want to have a hard finish, and it can be painted and varnished.

'Cooked' playdough

You will need:
   2 cups plain flour
   2 tablespoons cream of tartar
   1.5 cups water
   0.5 cup of salt
   1 tablespoon oil
   A few drops of food colouring
Method: Mix together flour and cream of tartar. Boil water, salt, oil and food colouring in a saucepan. Stir liquid into the flour, allow to cool, then knead until smooth. Cool further before letting children use it.

If you wrap this dough in a couple of polythene bags it will keep for some time in a fridge. Obviously, small children should be discouraged from eating this, though the high salt content and the cream of tartar usually ensure they only taste it once!

Uncooked playdough

(makes enough for 8-10 children)
You will need:
   4 cups plain flour
   2 cups water
   2 cups salt
   2 tablespoons cooking oil
   Food colouring
Method: Add salt to flour, and gradually add the water and oil, stirring constantly. When everything is well mixed, sprinkle work top with flour and knead dough. (This can be done in an electric mixer with a dough hook attachment.)

This dough will not last as long as the cooked variety but is fine in an emergency or if you have no cooking facilities.

to us and to God, if week after week we present them with dog-eared paper, a box of ill-assorted felt-tip pens (most of which don't work), broken lead pencils and blunt coloured ones? It doesn't take long to check materials at the end of the session, put the glue brushes or spreaders in a polythene bag to take home to wash if you can't do it where you meet, and to put everything back in its rightful place. That also saves the 'Where on earth are the scissors?' panic the following week.

What do I need?

Apart from saving things like used cereal packets, cardboard tubes, yoghurt pots and egg boxes, you will need to assemble the following basic equipment (depending to some extent on the age of your group): **white paper; coloured paper and card; sugar paper; felt-tip pens; colouring pencils; lead pencils; crayons; scissors** (if possible enough pairs for at least one between two); **an all-purpose glue such as PVA**, decanted into smaller pots. (The containers used for 35mm films are airtight once the lids are on firmly, but not very stable. I prefer to use the squat, screwtop jars in which moisturising cream and similar products are sold.) Good alternatives to PVA

glue are glue-sticks such as 'Pritt' or those sold for young children by Early Learning Centre where the glue is purple at first, so that children can see where they've glued, but dries colourless.

If you have space and time to paint, keep **paint brushes, sponges** for sponge-printing and **a selection of paints**. (Powder paint is cheapest but fiddly to mix and messy, so ready-mixed paint in litre containers is a good alternative.) If you keep paints in your equipment box or cupboard, it's worth also keeping **newspapers** for protecting tables and – for protecting children's clothes – **disposable polythene aprons** or polythene carrier bags with the handles at the sides (not in the middle); these can be cut across the bottom and used as tabard-type aprons. It's also worth keeping **washing-up liquid and cloths** for wiping down tables and mopping up spills.

Leaders will also find a **craft knife** (obtainable from art and hobby supplies shops) very useful, plus '**Blu-tack**', a roll of **sticky tape**, **sharper scissors** than the children's, **thin string and pegs** for hanging things to dry or display, **kitchen roll** and a large **box of tissues**, a **stapler, staples** and **a gadget for getting staples out**.

Where do I get all this?

If you know any teachers or playgroup leaders, ask them if there is an educational supplier in the area which sells biggish packs at a discount – many large towns have one. (NB Mail order educational suppliers tend to be very expensive.) Failing that, Early Learning Centre produces good quality, reasonably-priced equipment of the kind mentioned above, including paints, glue-spreaders, large packs of coloured paper, metallic card and scissors with interesting blades. Bigger branches of Boots (usually those with a childrenswear department) often sell good activity packs which include stencils, templates and packs of paper, and WH Smith also sells lots of reasonably-priced craft stuff, such as packs of lolly sticks for making lolly-stick puppets or things like large stars in gold and silver card, which are useful if you have a small group or not much time to cut things out beforehand.

Large hobby or craft shops can be expensive but it's worth looking round them. They often sell very interesting and useful specialised 'bits and pieces', unobtainable in chain stores, as well as things like 500g tins of glitter (imagine spilling that lot!). They often also have free information and 'how to' sheets.

Salt dough

(for 6-8 children)
You will need:
    3 cups plain flour
    1 cup salt
    1 cup water
    1 tablespoon cooking oil
Method: Mix all ingredients to form a dough and knead for a minute. Add a little more water if necessary (different brands and types of flour absorb different quantities of water). Cover with a damp cloth or cling film, or place in a polythene bag, and leave for 30 minutes before use.

Keep in a polythene bag to stop dough drying out and use within 24 hours.

This dough can be used in a similar way to baking clay, ie for models that you want to paint and varnish. It should be cooked in a slow oven – 100°C/210°F/Gas Mark 1, for about three hours.

COMMON SENSE SAFETY PRECAUTIONS

It goes without saying that parents expect, and have a right to expect, that when they entrust their children to a church group, those children will be cared for and protected. We need to ensure, therefore, that the environment in which they take part in craft activities is as safe as we can make it. Common sense precautions include having enough adult help and supervision. Very young children can be amazingly creative with any sort of equipment and even an innocent paper clip can be a hazard to a three year old if she swallows it, pokes it in her ear or up her nose. So be aware all the time of even *potential* hazards – a child can injure herself in the ten seconds when your back is turned – so always enlist extra help for craft activities.

→ Always have a basic first aid kit available.

→ Know where fire extinguishers, fire blankets and fire exits are.

→ Know the names of registered first-aiders in your church.

→ Make sure felt-tip pens are washable and non-toxic and have safety caps.

→ Discourage children from putting anything into their mouths, especially if they are walking about.

→ Don't allow young children to use sharp scissors but make sure the ones you provide for them do the job.

→ Never, ever leave under-fives alone in a room.

→ Never, ever take your eyes off children using or playing with water.

→ If activities involve water, have a mop handy – slippery floors can be lethal.

→ Don't allow younger children to use craft knives.

→ Don't allow older children to use craft knives unsupervised

→ Keep 'adult' equipment such as craft knives, matches and anything chemical, well out of reach and out of sight.

→ Keep electrical equipment, especially kettles and heaters, out of the way and don't have trailing flexes.

→ Don't allow children to rush around in a crowded room.

1 Multi-use resources

Even if you are unable to find an activity directly related to a specific story or topic, you can often devise an activity based on one of the multi-use resources below – banners, bookmarks, collages, cards, wheels, posters, puppets, models or mobiles. (Strictly speaking collage is a technique and can be used to make almost all the others listed, except puppets and models, but the term is also used for the finished product of the technique.) The notes and illustrations in this section are by no means exhaustive, just some basics to set you off.

COLLAGE/MONTAGE

These two terms are now used more or less interchangeably though originally they were slightly different. Both refer to a method of creating a picture or design using things like scraps of material or small pieces of paper, woodshavings, pasta or beads or seeds or... The possibilities are endless. The most appealing thing about collages is that you can suit the materials to the theme, so you could have a collage sheep made from strands of wool, or a harvest scene made from grains and seeds, or a seaside picture with shells and sand.

Collages can be big or small, simple or complex and are ideal as group or individual activities. All you need is glue and spreaders, a background sheet with a design sketched on it, and pieces of material to work with. The end result can be displayed as a picture or poster, or made into a card or banner.

See the suggestions for collages in other sections for specific examples eg 'Circle of Creation' in **God's world** or 'Water collage' in **Weather**.

MOBILES

Strictly speaking, a mobile should have several hanging items so suspended that the balance is perfect, but a) this is hard to achieve with a group of children all clamouring for help to finish their own masterpieces, and b) the term has come to be used for any craft design to be hung up for display. Again they are very useful resources and almost anything can be made into a mobile! For suspending items, a metal coathanger (the thinner the better) is very useful, especially as it already has a hanging loop. The hanger itself can be disguised by winding crepe paper, coloured sticky tape, shiny ribbon or tinsel, etc round it. Items can be suspended using fishing line, cotton, or fine wire. The illustration shows another way of making a simple mobile, by suspending items from a circle of card. See ideas for mobiles in **God's world** and **Pentecost**.

CARDS

A very versatile resource. Most children love making cards, especially if they are allowed to load them with glitter, stickers, etc. You will find ideas for cards in several sections. There is also a very comprehensive section on cards in *Here's One I Made Earlier*.

Cut out cards

Fold a sheet of paper into four and snip out shapes. Open up and write message. Fold up again to give away.

Printed cards

Cut potatoes in half and sculpt different shapes on the cut edge using a potato peeler. Dip into paint and print. When dry, write a message inside.

Weaving cards

Cut vertical slits on the front of the card. Cut brightly coloured strips and weave through slits. Cut strips to exact size and glue ends down. Open up and write message.

BANNERS

Banners are a bit like posters but are usually portable (good for processions) and have a background of cloth rather than card or paper. For young children it's easiest to glue shapes cut from fabric on to the background, though older ones might like to try sewing. As the illustration shows, even simple banners can be very effective.

For hanging banners, sew a hem about 10cm deep, top and bottom, and insert a piece of dowelling, then add a loop of cord to the top. For banners to be carried in a procession, you need hems at each side, with dowelling inserted vertically, so that two children can hold a pole at either side.

Sky banner

Paint a dark blue background. Create outlines of stars (see **Templates** section), moon and sun and paste onto card. Mix yellow paint and wallpaper adhesive (suitable only for older children, because of the fungicides some contain) and water. Paint the sun, moon and stars and sprinkle with glitter while wet. Paste onto banner.

POSTERS

Posters are usually a group activity, and the point about a poster is that it's meant to be seen – so it needs to be as big as is practicable. You can choose to make a poster of a memory verse, or a theme or a way of putting into practice something you've learned as a group, and you can print, paint or collage. The circular harvest poster illustrated combines several elements – it's an interesting shape, it has a verse, and it incorporates some of the teaching points.

A simpler type of 'poster' is shown in the washing line illustration at the top of the page, where the letters of the words 'Give thanks to the Lord' have been decorated individually and simply pegged to a line.

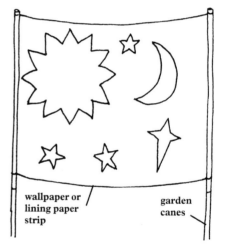

wallpaper or lining paper strip

garden canes

Earth banner

Paint the background blue and green as shown. Cut out three triangles from card, paint them grey with white tops for mountains. Cut two cloud shapes from blue paper. Bubble paint them white. Paste onto

Circular harvest poster

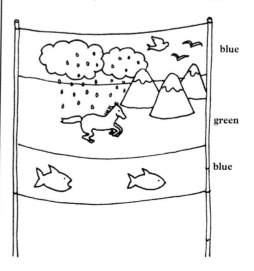

blue

green

blue

background, spread glue and shake on rice for rain/snow effect. Draw fish, birds and animals to paste onto the banner.

• Fill a small bowl with ready-mixed white powder paint and washing-up liquid. Using a straw, blow the mixture into bubbles. Wipe or lay the paper across the bubbles. NB Make sure that each child blows DOWN the straw rather than sucking up it.

People banner

Paint the background blue and green as shown. Draw lots of different types of people: young, old, royalty, multi-racial, etc (or cut out pictures from magazines). Paste figures onto background

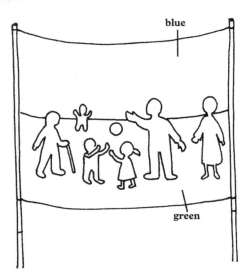

BOOKMARKS

These, like cards, can be all shapes, colours and sizes, made as gifts or for personal use, and often useful as an aid to remembering a special Bible verse.

See marbled bookmarks in **Bits and bobs**, for a special technique, but generally keep coloured card and means to decorate them, and maybe some embroidery thread to make tassels for the base.

PRINTING

This is really a technique but is in itself another versatile and ever-popular activity. We all like – literally – to make our mark!

You can print with almost anything that has a textured surface, but the most popular means of printing include potato prints, where a shape is cut into a halved potato (or other hard vegetable), and sponge printing. Thick poster paint is good, especially with young children (mix in a little washing-up liquid for easier cleaning up) but it's also possible to buy coloured inkpads, which are less messy. Older children might like to try some techniques used by interior decorators, eg 'ragging' where a design is made with a small piece of screwed-up cloth. Uses for printing activities include cards, bookmarks, borders for posters, flags and banners and

home-made wrapping paper. For printing activities you need the paint in very shallow containers, like old saucers or large plastic jar lids. You also need plenty of newspapers, soap and towels!

See 'Crowded Out' in **Easter** for an example of a potato print poster activity.

PUPPETS

There are endless varieties of simple puppets which you can make with children or as visual aids. The list below, and the illustrations showing how they are made are just a few, and you will find other examples in other sections.

Paper bag puppets

Use water-based felt pens (permanent markers will go through the paper) to draw the face and name of a character on one side of the paper bag. Draw the back of the head or the whole figure on the reverse side of the bag.

You can also draw towns or other items to illustrate your story.

Finger puppets

Cut two paper shapes for each puppet. Put a narrow band of paste along the edge except for the bottom and press shapes together firmly.

Draw features, hair, clothes, etc with felt-tip pens.

Wooden spoon puppet

On the back of the spoon, draw a face or attach a piece of paper with a face drawn on. Dress the puppet by attaching fabric, with rubber bands, at the neck for a robe and on the head for a headdress.

Paper people

1 Cut an A4 sheet of paper in half lengthwise and stick the ends together to make one long strip. Fold into eight sections concertina-style.

2 Make a template for the children to draw around. Cut out carefully, keeping folds at hands. Unfold with care and decorate as desired.

Other simple models or puppets can be made from wooden pegs (see 'Soldiers' in **Bible people**).

WHEELS

These can be used to retell a story to emphasise a teaching point for young children, eg 'God is with me everywhere', to depict practical applications of a memory verse on the 'cover' of the wheel, or as a prayer reminder. Wheels consist of two circles of card, joined at the centre by a butterfly fastener, so that the upper section, which has a segment cut out, can rotate. The upper section can be plain, or decorated, or have a memory verse printed on it. The lower section is divided into any suitable number of segments, from 2 to 8, and consists of pictures which are revealed gradually as the cutaway segment reaches them.

Matchbox puppet

Photocopy the face illustrated. Colour it in and paste it around the sleeve of a small matchbox. Cover the middle and index finger of one hand with a scarf or handkerchief. Slot the matchbox sleeve over the fingers.

Cylinder puppet

1 Cover the lower half of a cardboard cylinder with paper or fabric.
2 Copy the face onto a small circle of paper. Paste this onto the upper part of the cylinder.
3 Make a headdress to tie around the puppet using wool, ribbon or string.

Pipe cleaner puppets

1 Join two pipe cleaners together as shown.
2 Cut scraps of fabric.
3 Dress figures and add features by taping on paper faces and other items.

2 Advent and Christmas

DOES the thought of Christmas craft fill you with dread (glitter everywhere – again!), boredom (not *more* angels), or excitement (what shall we do *this* year?)? Yes, it's increasingly difficult to find new craft activities for Christmas, and often, by the time we in church get to them in Advent, playgroups and schools have been 'doing' Christmas since half-term and it's hard to compete!

Most schools and nurseries, though, won't have stressed the spiritual aspect of Christmas and that's our focus. If we can regain and retain that sense of awe at the mystery and wonder of the Christmas story and message, we shall transmit that to the children, however simple the Christmas craft we are engaged in.

Remember three things: first, part of the joy of Christmas, especially for children, is doing things the way we've done them before; second, activities which seem 'old hat' to us, are often new and rewarding to children; third, time goes faster as we get older so whilst last Christmas seems only a couple of weeks ago to us, to children it seems more like a hundred years since the last one! So, grab that glitter glue, dust off the doileys, sort out the stars, take a deep breath and look at the ideas in this section – you never know, you just might find something you haven't done or made before!

You will also find other craft activities appropriate to or adaptable for Christmas in the **Angels** and **Sheep and shepherds** sections, a craft prayer idea in **Prayer** and a Mexican star in **Bits and bobs**.

Craft activities involving lights or candles could be adapted for other light themes.

Christmas music

Tree shoot stuck in a cotton reel

Boxes in wrapping paper

Plasticine figures

Cut from old cards

Get ready for Jesus

Tin lid or cake board

ADVENT WREATH OR CROWN

Many churches and families make an advent wreath each year. Basically it consists of a ring of four candles, with a central, bigger candle of a contrasting colour. On the first Sunday in Advent, one candle is lit; on the second Sunday, two candles and so on, until on Christmas Day the central candle, representing Jesus, is lit too. The 'crown' illustrated shows an interesting variant of the Advent wreath – follow the instructions to make it with your group.

1 Write 'Get ready for Jesus' on a long strip of paper and stick it around the side of a tin lid (or on a cake board).

2 Add the candles, making sure that they are held securely in place with plasticine and also that they are well above the decorations so as to reduce the risk of fire.

3 Add other Christmas features as shown on the diagram.

Other adaptations of the advent wreath idea include:

Mini advent wreaths

These are made out of salt dough, plaited, baked and varnished or painted (optional) when cold. You need to make 4 holes with the base of a small candle, the size you intend to use, before baking the wreath, perhaps filling the holes with crumpled foil. After cooling the baked dough you may need to anchor the candles with Blu-tack or crumpled foil. The central candle can go in a piece of clay or plasticine.

Using foliage and 'oasis'

If you want to make a large one with your group (aged 7 upwards) for use in church, buy a special 'wreath base' from a florist. This has a ring of oasis bonded onto a polystyrene base. (NB Make sure you stand anything with foliage on a tray so that it can be watered.) Use lots of greenery, especially aromatic herbs like rosemary, berries and any winter-flowering shrubs you can find. The secret is to keep the foliage very short and tuck in lots of it so that the base is covered completely. Use fine hairpins to anchor things like ivy which have bendy stems. You will have to replace the flowers (winter jasmine for example) each week, but if you water the wreath regularly and spray the foliage, ivy, berries, rosemary and other evergreens will last through Advent. Children could make a smaller version using circles of oasis, and small candles. Remind them never to use candles or matches unsupervised, however, and never to leave a lit candle unattended.

An old 'Blue Peter' version

Use 4 large potatoes wrapped in silver foil with a florist's candleholder in each, to make the basic crown. Decorate each foiled potato with greenery, small Christmas baubles, pine cones, etc. (Wrap florist's or thin garden wire round items you want to stick into the potato.)

5 DOOR ADVENT CALENDAR

This simple calendar can be made by children and one door opened each Sunday in Advent.

1 Cut a sheet of Christmas wrapping paper to A4 size and glue it to a plain A4 sheet of paper. Cut 5 doors as shown – this is best done with a craft knife and adult supervision.

2 Place another sheet of paper underneath.

Open the doors and mark their positions on the lower sheet.

3 Photocopy the 5 pictures and colour them.

4 Glue the pictures in the correct order on the lower sheet.

5 Finally, glue together around the edges of the page. Close the doors and fix in position with a tiny piece of tape.

ADVENT BOXES

Use a cardboard egg tray or a seed tray with at least 24 tiny compartments. Into each compartment put a small gift such as sweets, or instructions such as 'Sing a Christmas carol'. Cover each gift with a scrunched-up piece of tissue, and then with a small, sticky label, previously numbered 1 to 24. Open one compartment on each day of Advent.

STAR AND CROWN ADVENT DECORATION

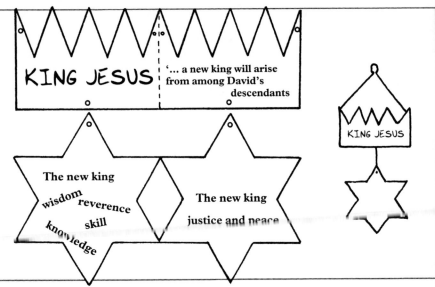

See illustration. The crown is a reminder that Jesus is King, while the star of David reminds us that Jesus was descended from King David. The writing on the star includes qualities which Isaiah prophesied Jesus would have.

Draw a crown and star as shown. Cut around the shape of the crown, fold it in half along the dotted line and paste the two sides together. Cut out the two stars and paste them together back to back. Decorate the crown and star with glitter or foil shapes and thread the pieces together as shown.

CANDLE PICTURE

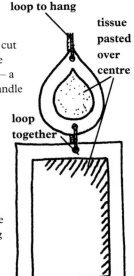

From sugar paper, cut out a simple candle shape in two parts – a rectangle for the candle itself and a flame shape. Cut out the centre of each shape (see illustration), then paste a piece of coloured tissue paper on the reverse to cover the whole shape. Hang in the window for the light to shine through.

"I am the light of the world"

CANDLE CARDS

Fold a rectangle of card in half. Draw a candle on the front and write an appropriate verse along the bottom, beneath the candle. Cut out a flame shaped hole. Cut a circle of card for the candle 'rays' and colour with mixed flame colours. Attach the circle behind the flame cut-out using a paper

PROTECTIVE CANDLEHOLDERS

Make cardboard discs to protect hands from hot wax when carrying candles (see centre illustration). For added effect, cover the discs with silver foil. Use long candles.

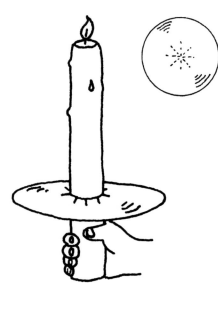

Half a cardboard tube for 3D effect

fastener. Then cut a small semicircle out of the side of the card as a finger hole to turn the wheel and make the flame flicker.

Decorate candle by:
- colouring it in.
- pasting on decorative paper, eg Christmas wrapping paper.
- decorating half a cardboard tube and pasting it on so that you've got a 3D candle.

FLAMING TORCHES

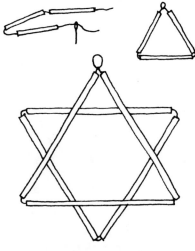

Uses: *Christmas services; link to the story of Gideon*

Sometimes a Christmas service, an evening carol service for example, involves a lighted procession. Here is a way to provide safe lights with the atmosphere of a candlelit procession:

Tape a tall crown of flame-coloured tissue or crepe paper around the light on a torch, then gather the top together with sticky tape to form a cone shape.

STAR OF DAVID

You will need:
  6 drinking straws
  A darning needle
  A length of strong thread for each child
  A tube of all-purpose glue

Thread three straws and tie together tightly to make a triangle (see illustration). Do the same with the other three straws. Place one triangle over the other to make a Star of David and fix it in place with three spots of glue. Hang the stars from a length of tinsel or spray with gold or silver paint before mounting on a card.

CHRISTMAS STORY MODELS AND SHOE BOX STABLE SCENE

See illustration. The cardboard tube figures can be part of a traditional 'crib' scene or used as finger puppets.

1 Make a stable scene from a shoe box: turn the box on its side and cut off the top. Paint the box inside and out. When dry, put straw or hay on the floor.

2 Make the figures: roll up a piece of card of the colour required (suggested depth 10cm). Tape the seam to secure. Tape or staple the top, squashing it slightly. Add arms and face cut from card. Add extra details for different characters (see illustration).

3 Make a crib: use a small matchbox painted brown or black. Fill it with straw or hay pieces. Dress half of a lolly stick to represent baby Jesus.

SHEPHERD CHRISTMAS CARDS

Enlarge a simple design, such as the shepherds illustrated here, and colour it in or collage with self-adhesive stars, striped wrapping paper or fabric, and pipe-cleaners for shepherds' crooks. Sheep made from cotton wool balls dipped into white paint could be added and their features drawn on in felt-tip pen once the paint is dry.

CRACKERS

You will need:
Short cardboard rolls
Paste
Pieces of crepe paper 30cm long and 20cm wide
Elastic bands
Gummed shapes and glitter, etc for decoration
Plus a small surprise present to put in your cracker!

1 Place the roll on one of the long sides of the paper and spread paste across the middle as shown in the diagram.
2 Roll up the tube in the paper.
3 Pinch in one end and put an elastic band round it.
4 Put in a sweet, toy or small gift and then pinch in the other end with an elastic band.
5 Decorate your cracker and give it to someone as a Christmas surprise!

TWIGGY TWINKLES

This is a simple Christmas mobile for the very youngest children.
You will need:
Pre-cut star shapes in different sizes with holes punched for hanging
Shiny ribbon
A bare twiggy branch
Materials for decorating stars
Once stars are decorated, loop the ribbon through the holes, knot and let children hang them on the twigs. Position the twigs where they will catch the light and the breeze or over a radiator where the stars will move in the warm air.

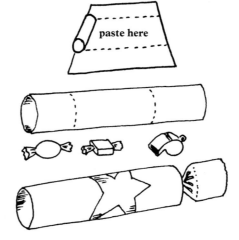

paste here

CHRISTMAS POSTER

(for young children)
Use a large piece of card for the background and stick as many traditional Christmas symbols as you can around the sides and lower half (old Christmas cards would be a good source of suitable pictures). At the centre of the top edge paste a decorated star, and below it, but in a central position, paste a picture of Jesus in the manger, perhaps with some pieces of straw. In the space at the side, write, 'Above all, Jesus.'

KING PICTURES

(suitable for Epiphany)
Draw simple bold outlines (like gingerbread people) and let children make them into 'kings' by adding sparkly fabric, glitter, bright tissue squares, foil, sequins, etc. (This activity could be adapted for older children by using a slightly more sophisticated template for the outlines.)

CROWNS

Give each child a strip of metallic card long enough to go round his/her head, plus at least 5cm overlap. Provide materials to decorate the crowns – self-adhesive shapes, scrunched-up tissue paper, shiny fabric, or metallic wrapping paper. Staple or tape to fit head when finished. (If you use staples, stick a piece of sticky tape across the staple afterwards to prevent scratches.)
See also also **Hats and headgear** section.

MANGER CHRISTMAS CARD

This simple card will give enormous satisfaction to the youngest children. Make sure you have lots of spares, everything ready beforehand and plenty of adult help – it's amazing what under-5s can do with what appears to an adult to be a completely straightforward activity! As an alternative to the leaf shapes, if you have access to an educational supply shop, you could buy a pack of holly leaf and berry gummed shapes.

1 Copy the picture of the baby in the manger, below. Glue it on the centre front of a card, leaving plenty of room around it.
2 Cut leaf shapes in various shades of green. Let the children glue these around the picture to form a Christmas wreath, as shown.
3 Make berries by drawing them with felt-tip pen or paint, or by adding a few self-adhesive circle stickers coloured red.

3-D cards

You will need:

Christmas wrapping paper with a
frequently repeated pattern
Glue
Card
Double-sided sticky pads

1 Choose part of the wrapping paper, cut it
   out and stick it on the card.
2 Decide which parts you want to make
   stand out. Cut out these parts from
   another repeat of the pattern.
3 Use small bits of double-sided sticky pads
   (available from stationers) to stick them
   over the pattern on the card.
4 Repeat this so that some parts stand out
   even more.

(See **Angels** section for a similar activity.)

CHRISTMAS STARS

   Provide star shapes in yellow, silver or gold
card – use the star templates at the back of
the book to make your own. If you want to
hang them, punch a hole in the top before
they are decorated. Use collage materials
such as pasta shapes, cellophane or metallic
sweet wrappings, and pieces of yellow or
white drinking straws. Add glitter if you
wish. Use as tree or window decorations.

BOTTLE PUPPETS

You can make as many of these as you wish
– they can be used to tell the story, or in a
Christmas crib scene or tableau.

You will need:

Empty plastic drinks bottles of various
   sizes
Cotton wool
Elastic bands
Card and felt-tip pens
Scraps of fabric
Wool and cotton wool for hair and clothes
Something to weight the bottles (sand is
   quietest!)

To make a basic figure:

1 Fill a clean plastic bottle with a few
   beans or a handful of sand, to weigh it
   down. Make a pad of cotton wool over
   the bottle top. Cover with a circle of
   plain fabric. Hold in place with an elastic
   band.
2 Cut out a face (see pics below) and stick
   in place. Make a cloak from a strip of
   fabric and gather at the neck.

Mary

Elizabeth

Zechariah

Joseph

Gabriel

Jesus

BELL MOBILE OR TREE DECORATION

Follow the instructions to make this. Adults should make the holes in the base of the yoghurt pots in advance, using something like a hot darning or knitting needle. (Make sure you protect your hands with an oven glove.) Bells of the kind illustrated are obtainable from educational suppliers or from WH Smith or hobby shops.

You will need:
 Yoghurt pots
 Small bells
 String
 Wire coat hangers
 Collage or printing materials
1 Make a small hole in the base of the pot.
2 Hang a bell on a piece of string (or ribbon). Tie a large knot 5cm above bell.
3 Push loose ends of string through the hole in the pot.

4 Let the children decorate the outside of the pot with stickers, paint, glitter, etc.
5 To make a tree decoration, tie the loose ends of the string to make a hanging loop.
6 To make a mobile, hang several bells from wire coat hangers. Wrap the wire with ribbon, tinsel, or crepe paper strips.

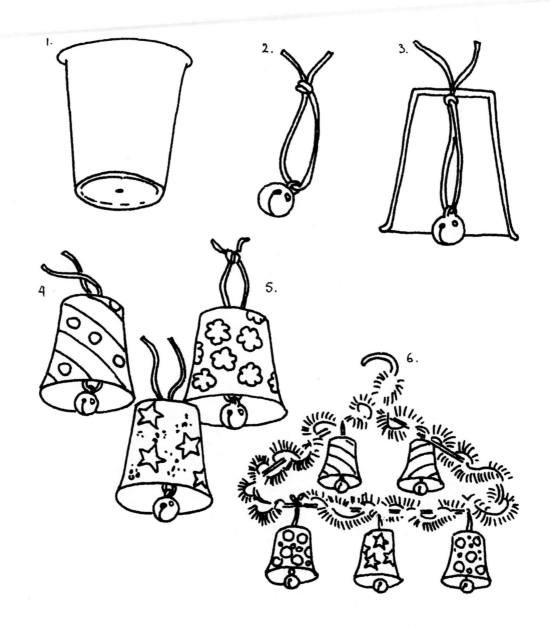

3 Easter

H E is risen – alleluia! Easter week, especially Easter Sunday, is both the climax of the church's year and the focus of the Christian's faith, for as Paul memorably puts it in his letter to the Corinthians, `... if Christ has not been raised, your faith is futile; you are still in your sins. ... But Christ has indeed been raised from the dead ...' (1 Corinthians 15:17-20).

None of us can fully grasp the significance of the cross, and the horror of the crucifixion is difficult to tackle with young children. There is also the danger that the Easter message can, like the Christmas story, become so familiar that its impact is lost. This is where craft activities come into their own. Children are much more likely to enter into something of the excitement of Palm Sunday and catch the joy of the resurrection by participating in craft activities which focus on the Easter message, than just by 'hearing the story'. So here you will find several simple 'drama' ideas which use puppets and models, as well as ideas for cards and Easter decorations.

PALM SUNDAY PUPPETS AND BASEBOARD

Making the baseboard could be a group activity, but children may well want to make a donkey and a person puppet each! The people puppets could be the crowd or Jesus' disciples, depending on how many you are able to make.

Baseboard

Cover base (strong corrugated card or softboard) with newspaper and glue. Screw up newspaper and cover with newspaper strips and plenty of glue. (Use wallpaper paste only with older children because of the fungicide contained in many pastes. With younger children use flour and water paste or PVA glue thinned slightly with warm water.)

Make houses from small cardboard boxes. Cut down sides and turn box inside out to make without painting. Stick together again with sticky tape inside.

Paint the board green with a brown road when the glue is completely dry.

Note: To change baseboard to an Easter garden, remove houses. Paint a cave entrance on one of the hills and put a suitable stone nearby. Put three crosses on a distant hill. Decorate the garden with twigs, blossom and flowers, real or made from tissue.

Donkey

Enlarge the donkey pictures. Colour in or collage and cut out. Stick on opposite sides of a cardboard tube. Strengthen the legs with strips of card going inside and across the tube.

Puppets

Use cardboard tubes. Draw a face at the top, leaving room for a headdress. Dress with fabric rectangles (tied on with wool for headdress, pasted on for robe).

17

EASTER STORY CARD

Photocopy the illustration opposite and trim the edges. Fold in half lengthways down the centre dotted line so that the pictures are on the outside. Then fold each end into the centre along the shorter dotted lines, so that the blank space (marked 0) is on the outside of the card. Cut the slit lines then slot one into another so that the 'holly leaf' shape on the front is complete. When opened, the card reveals an empty tomb, joyful women and a stunned guard. Use the card to tell the story. The card may be coloured before or after folding.

EASTER BUTTERFLY CARDS

Advance preparation: save and wash eggshells, crush into smallish pieces and colour them by mixing small amounts in a jar with a few drops of food colouring. Make several different colours. Trace or photocopy butterfly shapes (see template) and cut out. Put strong glue onto the butterfly shapes and sprinkle the coloured eggshell fragments on top. Press gently to ensure that eggshells stick, then shake off any excess. Mount (by gluing) the butterflies onto prepared cards and write an Easter greeting inside or on the back.

This activity is also suitable for topics linked with creation and the world that God has made.

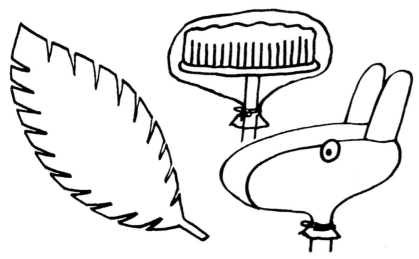

EASTER CARD

Photocopy the card illustration and stone onto thin card if possible (pasting a paper copy onto card can result in creasing of the paper). If you do this as a group activity, provide envelopes of the correct size for children to put their finished cards into.

Cut out the entrance to the tomb. Then colour in the card and the stone. Attach the stone to the card with a paper fastener at X so that it can be moved over the tomb and rolled away again.

Inside the card, write the message, 'JESUS IS RISEN' so that when the stone is rolled back, the words can be read inside the tomb. Add your own Easter greetings. Pop the card in an envelope and give it to a friend.

PALM SUNDAY DONKEY HOBBYHORSE AND PALMS

Use the background leaf as a template to make paper palm leaves from green crepe or sugar paper, or even from newspaper. (See also 'Flag prayers' in **Prayer** section.) Follow the instructions given to make a hobbyhorse donkey from a long-handled broom.

1 Cover a brush end with white, brown or grey paper or fabric. Secure by tying with wool or string or with sticky tape.

2 Turn the brush sideways and stick on ears at the sides, using the same paper or fabric as the head, backed on to card. Cut out card circles for eyes and stick on to the sides in front of ears.

HAPPY EASTER

Why not read the Easter story for yourself in Matthew 28:1-10?

Fold

Cut out this piece

CROWDED OUT

This activity points up the difference between the crowd shouting in praise of Jesus on Palm Sunday and shouting 'Away with him' a few days later. Make two crowd pictures by potato printing, as shown in illustration. Make a supply of speech bubbles. On one crowd picture put a speech bubble saying 'Jesus is King!' and on the other, one saying 'Kill him!' Children could use the extra speech bubbles to put modern sayings for and against Jesus, on the two pictures.

1 Cut a potato in half.
2 Use a blunt knife to gouge out holes for a mouth and eyes.
3 Dip into thick poster paint.
4 Print a crowd of people.

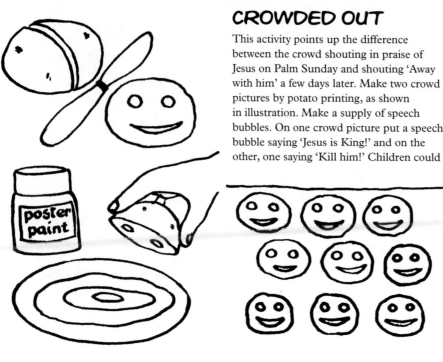

MOVING EASTER STORY PICTURE

Photocopy one copy of the illustration for each child. Cut out and colour in panels A and B. Then cut along the dotted lines marked on panel A. Thread panel B through these two slits so that the three pictures appear in the middle of panel A as they are pulled through the gap.

Tip: For extra strength paste panel A on to a piece of thin card and then cut the slits through both paper and card.

EASTER TREES

Photocopy the Easter shapes, cut them out and decorate them as desired, or use shapes cut from old Easter cards. Attach to lengths of coloured embroidery silk and display hung from leafy or flowering branches in a vase (see illustration).

EASTER EGG CRAFT IDEAS

Decorated eggs

Decorate hardboiled eggs using felt-tip pens, self-adhesive stickers, vegetable dyes, etc to make them distinctive. Older children might like to depict part of the Easter story or make their eggs into characters from the Easter story.

Eggshell flower arrangement

Put a small piece of Oasis (green porous block used by flower arrangers) into an eggshell. Because this is quite fragile, anchor it securely by setting it in an eggcup, the top from an aerosol can, or a section of cardboard tubing. Add to the Oasis twigs, sprigs of greenery and small flowers – real or artificial – to make an Easter decoration symbolising new life. (For under 5s, adapt the idea, using Oasis in a mousse or yoghurt pot, which you may have to weight down with a few small stones before inserting the Oasis.)

Eggshell heads

Decorate an empty eggshell (broken side up) with a face design. Put a piece of damp kitchen towel or some compost into the shell and sprinkle with grass or cress seeds. Keep seeds moist so that they grow as 'hair'.

UPPER ROOM SHOEBOX THEATRE

Follow illustration to make the theatre for use with 'witnesses' stick puppets.
Make the disciples' room from a cardboard box. Put the open side to the front. Cut away one third of the flat roof. Cut some windows and a door. Paint or paper the interior.

WITNESSES STICK PUPPETS

Use the templates provided opposite to make stick puppets for the Easter story, especially the resurrection appearances of Jesus in the upper room and elsewhere. These puppets/templates can be used in two ways –either in a shoebox theatre (see following activity), in which case the sticks should project above the puppets' heads (as in illustration), or as conventional stick puppets with the puppets at the top of the sticks.

These templates could also be used for other NT stories.

SWIZZLE STICKS

You will need:
- Thin garden canes
- Glue
- Card
- Felt-tip pens

Cut out two squares of card. Draw a picture of Jesus on the first square of card and a picture of a locked door on the second. (Alternatively photocopy the pictures and mount onto card.) Glue the pictures to either side of a length of garden cane. When the swizzle sticks are rolled briskly between the fingers, Jesus should appear in front of the locked door.

Soldiers

Two Marys

Angel

Templates for
witnesses stick puppets

Thomas

Disciples

Jesus

23

4 Pentecost (Whitsun)

PENTECOST – the birthday of the church! At Pentecost we celebrate the fulfilment of Jesus' promise that God would send the Holy Spirit to be with us for ever. It's an exciting story, an exciting festival and one at which we often talk about the symbols of the Holy Spirit: the dove which descended on Jesus at his baptism; the wind that 'blows wherever it wishes'; the tongues of flame which appeared on the heads of the believers when the Holy Spirit came. These symbols remind us that the Holy Spirit, invisible yet powerful, brings peace and energises us for service – and whichever symbol you choose to focus on, you will find craft ideas here for you to use.

BANNER 1 – GENTLE DOVES

Use the template provided and cut out several doves, which can be coloured in 'gentle' blues, mauves, greys, creams and pearly pinks, or covered in overlapping ovals of pale tissue paper. Stick or staple these to a fabric or card background and attach a verse about the Holy Spirit before displaying it.

BANNER 2 - DOVES

Use the tessellating bird template to make a more stylised design on your banner, explaining that one of the things the Holy Spirit does is to make us all fit together in God's family.

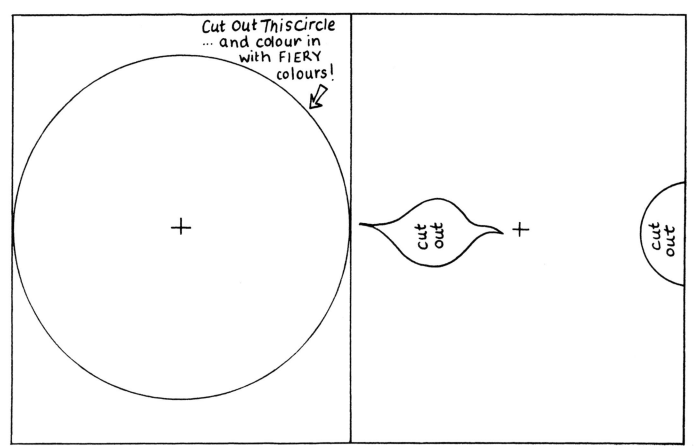

Cut out This Circle ... and colour in with FIERY colours!

cut out

cut out

FLAME CARDS

Photocopy the design onto thin card, perhaps in red, orange or yellow. Cut out the shaded flame-shaped section and the indent, using a craft knife, and make small holes at the crosses. Cut along the straight centre line and cut out the large circle. If you have used white card, colour the circle in fiery colours (wax crayons blend best).

Fasten the circle behind the rectangle through the holes at the crosses, using a split pin or 'butterfly' fastener. The circle can then be turned at the indent, changing the colour of the flame.

Write the verse on the card as shown: Jesus said, 'God will send you another helper who will be with you for ever.' (John 14:16 GNB)

Jesus ◊ said...
God will send you another helper who will be with you for ever.
John 14:16 GNB

FLAME BADGES

Use the flame templates to make badges as reminders of the Holy Spirit's promise to be with us for ever. Use red, orange or yellow card, or colour in. Paste the smaller flame onto the larger one. Attach a safety pin to reverse using sticky tape.

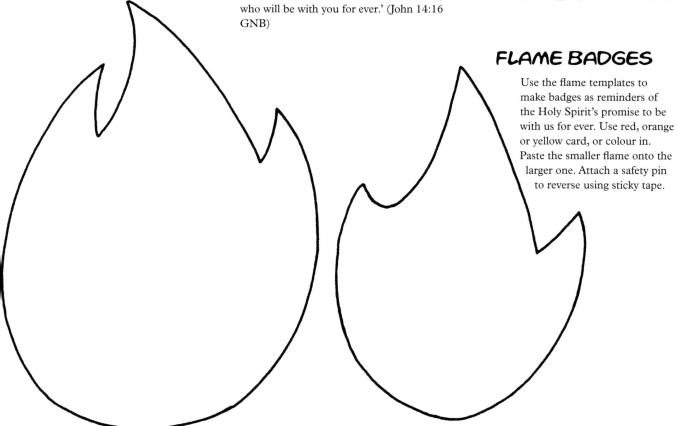

25

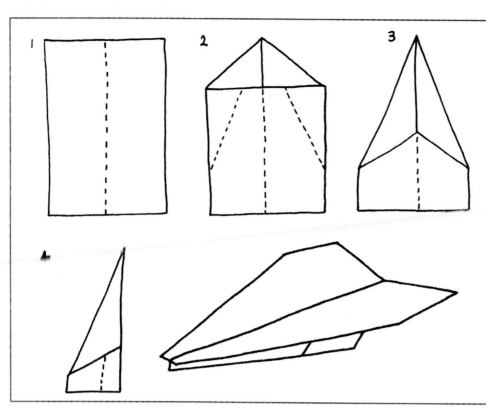

GLIDERS

Make gliders as shown in illustration. Link to the power of the Holy Spirit by explaining to your group that they are the ones who provide the power for the gliders to fly.

1 Take a rectangle of newspaper 20cm x 30cm (approx) and fold in half lengthwise. Flatten it out with crease up.

2 Fold over top corners to meet at centre line.

3 Fold over sides also to meet at centre line.

4 To make the keel, turn over and fold one side back at an angle to centre line. To make secure, staple the keel together and make firm folds. For safety, snip off the sharp point at the nose.

BREEZE BALL

Follow the directions to make this breeze ball. (Use a craft knife to pre-cut triangles for younger children.) Warn against playing with this near a road as it rolls very fast and is tempting to chase.

1 Cut out a circle 12-14cm in diameter and mark up as shown, writing an appropriate verse around the edge.

2 Carefully cut along the twelve solid lines starting from the centre. (Fold along one of the lines and snip to start, or use a craft knife.)

3 Fold alternate triangles up and down, as shown, all around the circle. There must be 6 triangles pointing each way (6 up, 6 down).

4 Drop the ball on the ground where a breeze can catch it, and watch it roll along.

DOVE MONEY-BOX

Use the template to make boxes in which to save for some special project at church, reminding children that the Holy Spirit gives us all gifts with which to serve God and other people.

To make your box:

1 Enlarge the template on a photocopier and cut out. Colour in the heart and the dove.

2 Cut out the heart, the dove, and the money box along the thick lines.

3 Cut carefully along the thick line which forms the slit in the top of the money box.

4 Fold along the dotted lines on the money box.

5 Glue tabs A, B and C in place under the base.

6 Glue tabs D, E and F in place under the top of the box.

7 Finally, put glue carefully on tab G and slide carefully into place inside the box.

8 Glue the heart and the dove to the two circles on the sides of the money box.

FLAME PRAYERS MOBILE

Use the template below to cut out flame shapes in fiery colours on which prayers can be written. Attach the prayers to a circle of card reading, 'Holy Spirit, please help...' or suspend from cotton to display.

Other uses: *These 'flame' ideas and templates could also be used for banners, bookmarks or headbands, and with other Bible stories featuring fire: Moses and the burning bush; Shadrach, Meshach and Abednego in the fiery furnace; Elijah on Mount Carmel; the burning coal which touched Isaiah's lips in the temple; the chariots of fire which Elijah and Elisha saw; the story of Samson. The flame templates could also be used to make a montage of the burning bush or the fiery furnace, using red, yellow, gold and orange tissue or crepe paper. The candle card could be adapted for use at Christmas or in any topic about light.*

SEALING RINGS

(see Ephesians 1:13)

You will need:

Plasticine

Objects for pressing in designs

Wax candles and matches or sealing wax

1 Roll plasticine into a sausage shape, but thicker in the middle.
2 Bend round the ends to make a ring.
3 Flatten the thick part and press in a design.

To make a seal:

Take great care and make sure the children do too. Hot wax can burn.

1 Position a length of ribbon.
2 Drip on some sealing or candle wax.
3 Allow it to harden slightly.
4 Press the ring down – not too hard – and remove cleanly.
5 Allow wax to harden.

Get everyone to make first a ring with a symbol or letter to show that the thing sealed belongs to them. Give each child a card on which to draw a self-portrait, sign their name and add a ribbon and their seal. Seal symbols might include a flame, a cross or the first initial of the child's name. Have ready cards or posters with the words 'The Holy Spirit – God's way of saying, "You're mine"' already written on them. Posters could have a long ribbon down one side and the whole group could add their seals.

KITE COLLAGE/ PRAYER POSTER

Provide a number of different kite shapes for decoration then fix them all to a 'sky' background and attach real string or twine, perhaps with bunting. Write on a verse about the wind of the Spirit, or let people write their own prayers on the kites before adding them to the poster.

WINDMILLS

Use the template provided (or see page 38 in *Here's One I Made Earlier*) for a variation on this simple windmill. Photocopy one for each child. After colouring, cut out and along diagonal lines. Bend marked corners over to centre and fix with pin onto stick or strong drinking straw. Cover sharp end of pin with plasticine or similar.

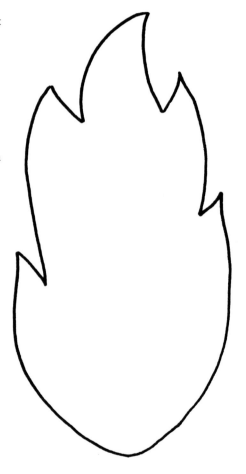

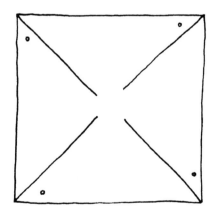

5 Mothering Sunday

WHEN my children were still quite young, we had a bit of a campaign about turning off lights, not wasting water by leaving taps running and so on, and they had clearly got the message: on Mothering Sunday morning they proudly appeared bearing a tray containing cornflakes, a mug of tea, and a boiled egg and told me, 'We remembered what you said about not wasting things, Mummy – we made your tea with the water we'd boiled the egg in.'

Sadly, Mothering Sunday – the middle Sunday in Lent – has, like other festivals, been hijacked by commercial interests, but most churches still mark the occasion by arranging for children to give small gifts such as flowers, cards or something they have made. In this section you will find suggestions for some simple inexpensive gifts which will give pleasure to givers and recipients.

If you prefer an edible gift, look in the **Recipe** section! You may also find suitable ideas in **Bits and bobs**.

MAKING POT-POURRI

A very simple recipe for pot-pourri is as follows. Mix together:

- 250g/8oz dried lavender
- 25g/1oz dried thyme
- 25g/1oz dried mint
- 15g/0.5oz salt
- 15g/0.5oz ground cloves
- 15g/0.5oz ground caraway

Place a handful of the mixture in the centre of a square of pretty fabric (cutting this with pinking shears will give an attractive decorative edge) and close into a bag with a thin elastic band. Tie a thin ribbon in a co-ordinating colour round the bag to hide the elastic band.

PAPER POSIES

Follow the directions to make simple posies for children to give to their mothers. The flower shapes can be decorated with paints, felt-tips, sticky shapes, sequins, material, foil, lace, etc. (Other flowers to make can be found in the **God's world** section.)

1 Cut two flower shapes from coloured card (see template).
2 Tape a plastic straw to the back of one shape and paste the other shape over the straw so that it is sandwiched between them.
3 Paste a circle of foil at the centre of each flower shape.
4 Put two or three flowers through the centre of a paper doily and cover the stems to make a posy.

MOTHERING SUNDAY CARDS

Have materials available for children to design their own cards (see illustration). For something a little bit different, you could get children to draw (or paste on a cut-out shape of) a cup and saucer, with the caption, 'Let me make you a cup of tea.' Inside, attach a teabag on a string!

POT-POURRI GIFTS

Follow the instructions here for a simple gift – remember that sometimes it's best to make gifts like these a week before, so that children have them ready for the morning of Mothering Sunday. If net is not available you could use coloured cellophane or crepe paper, but would then need to make sure the ends of the flower wire were covered with tape to prevent them piercing the paper.

1 Make the flower centre by looping lengths of flower ribbon, securing each loop with a twist of flower wire.
2 Cut two circles of Breton nylon net, 25cm and 28cm in diameter. Two colours of net and ribbon makes a more attractive flower. Place a spoonful of potpourri in centre, insert the wire end of the flower centre, fold up net and secure with an elastic band.
3 Cover elastic band with ribbon tied in a loop for hanging.

6 God's world

WE live in a wonderful and beautiful world! Despite our greed, waste and despoiling of much that God has made, the natural world still reflects his glory and points us to the Creator who gives and sustains life. Every 'natural world' programme on television is an awesome reminder of our amazing God! Every new baby, as well as each new scientific discovery about the way in which our brains are programmed or our bodies work, is a reminder that we are 'fearfully and wonderfully made' in God's image! So our love of making things – of craft activities – is an outworking of that creativity which is part of being human and of being made in God's image. Everything we make with the children in our groups is an expression of this God-given creativity – it's a stimulating thought.

Children are fascinated by the world around them, especially that of animals and creepy-crawlies, so there are several activities based on these, most of which are suitable for even the youngest children. (There are other activities in **Birds** and **Weather** and body links in **Hands, feet and faces**.) Don't forget leaf-printing (see instructions below) and bark rubbing, as well as collages and even models made from natural materials – seed heads, grasses, pine cones, wood-shavings, bark, moss, straw and so on.

ALL CREATION MOBILE

This is a group activity and can last for several sessions. **You will need:** thread; hole punch and needles; felt-tip pens or paints and brushes; fabric; shiny and coloured paper; scissors; letter templates or stencils; large circles of card for the world; a rectangle of very thick card for the header; wire or thin sticks (such as plant support sticks) for cross pieces; cotton wool for clouds; glitter; glue pens; gold and silver foil for moon, stars and sun; scraps of fabric including fur fabric; animal pictures; mail order catalogues with pictures of domestic appliances and computers, etc; card for children to cut out pictures of themselves. Use the illustration as a guide to make a mobile as a reminder that it is still God's world. The verse you choose,

such as 'All things were created by God's Son and everything was made for him' (Colossians 1:16) forms the strip from which all the other things are suspended.

CREATION MOBILE

Enlarge the illustrations on to strips of paper (or draw your own) and let children colour them before attaching them to a wire coathanger. This could be a group or an individual activity.

All things were created by God's Son and everything was made for him

CIRCLE OF CREATION

This activity is very adaptable. You could cut out a huge circle for the group to complete as a creation collage, using pictures from gardening and shopping catalogues, or fabric and natural materials. The large version, completed, could be displayed as a poster or banner.

Alternatively you could give each child a smaller version to complete by collaging (in which case just give them the circle divided into blank segments) or by drawing or colouring (in which case give each child a large photocopy of the illustration). You could also make this into a 'wheel' activity as follows: use a butterfly fastener to attach a black circle with one-eighth cut away, on top of the picture circle, for children to retell the story of creation.

Divide the circle into 8 equal parts and then the north-north-east segment into two equal halves (see illustration). Numbering clockwise from the top (or 12 o'clock), you have segments 1 through 8.

➜ **Section 1a**: Yellow = day
➜ **Section 1b**: Dark blue or black = night
➜ **Section 2a**: Pale blue = sky
➜ **Section 2b**: Light green = dry land
➜ **Section 3**: Pictures of plants, fruit and vegetables = creation of plant life
➜ **Section 4**: Near centre of circle - pale blue background with sun; near outside of circle - blue or black background with moon and stars = creation of sun and moon
➜ **Section 5**: Blue or green background with sea creatures = creation of marine life
➜ **Section 6**: Pictures of birds drawn or pasted on = creation of flying creatures
➜ **Section 7**: Pictures of animals pasted on = creation of animal kingdom
➜ **Section 8**: Draw outlines or paste on pictures of people = creation of man.

JUNK MODEL CREATIONS

Provide junk modelling material such as cartons, packets, bottles, lids, etc, scissors and glue. Invite children to create something from the junk. Ask how it feels to make something from junk, then point out that God created from nothing.

LEAF AND CATERPILLAR

Cut out a large leaf shape from green card or paper for each child (older children could do this for themselves). Punch a few holes in the leaf shape and tear away small pieces at the edge to suggest the caterpillar has been eating it, as above. Cut caterpillar shapes from felt or from cream or green card (a different shade from the leaf), and mark features with felt-tips or adhesive shapes. Remind children that caterpillars are usually found on the underside of leaves, then paste caterpillar to the back of leaf so that it can be partially seen through the holes - though younger children may prefer to stick the caterpillar to the front of the leaf.

GIANT CATERPILLAR

Collect egg boxes and tape together, or link with string, several humped sections. Paint the circles on top of each section green or brown, or paste on circles of coloured paper. At the front of the first section cut a slit and blow up a round green balloon to a suitable size for a head. Tie the neck of the balloon so that it will fit in the slit you have made.

Add facial features and secure the head in place with tape such as masking tape. Put strips of card underneath the egg boxes for feet, gluing or taping them into position.

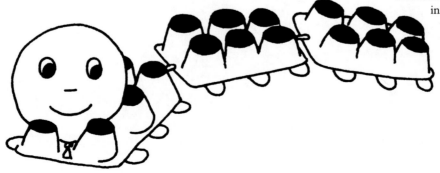

BUTTERFLY PAINTINGS

Give each child a large butterfly shape cut from paper. Drop blobs of paint onto one half of the shape. Fold butterfly in half down the centre, ie symmetrically, pressing the blank side lightly onto the painted side, then open out to give a symmetrical pattern. Leave to dry. Punch a hole at the top and thread a piece of yarn or cotton through the hole to suspend the butterfly.

BUTTERFLY LOLLY STICK OR FINGER PUPPET

1 Cut out the template shape above in thin coloured card or sugar paper.
2 Paste on coloured and/or shiny shapes to decorate.
3 For a finger puppet, tape a pipe cleaner to the reverse and wrap around a finger (but not too tightly!). For a lolly-stick puppet, tape a lolly stick to the back and make the butterfly move.

FINGERPRINT PICTURES

Remind children that we are all unique – no one has fingerprints exactly like ours! Provide finger paints or a water-based stamp pad and let children make pictures from their fingerprints, eg caterpillars, tadpoles, birds – extra features can be added in felt tip pen.

LEAFPRINTS

Find some good-sized leaves and cover one side in a fairly thick layer of paint. Place face downwards on the background, and if possible roll over them firmly with a rolling pin/jam jar, so that the finer details of the leaf as well as the outline are printed. Peel leaf off carefully and repeat.

BUTTERFLY AND CATERPILLAR POSTER

Uses: *topics about change, eg story of Zacchaeus.*
See illustration. You will need a large backing sheet, and butterfly templates of different sizes, preferably in different coloured card or sugar paper. Let each child decorate a butterfly and also design and make a caterpillar. All the creatures are then stuck to the backing sheet – butterflies at the top, caterpillars at the bottom – which has in the centre the caption, 'Jesus can change your life'.

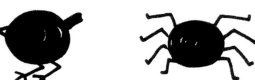

SPIDER'S WEB

Cut a piece of white paper approximately 21cm x 21cm. Cut out a small 'door' in the centre. Let children draw lines for the web (see illustration) – younger children will need help with this. The webs can be decorated with glitter paint or glitter glue, or paste sprinkled with dry glitter, fine sand, or sawdust. Make spider shapes out of black felt or paper (again, younger children will need help) and glue the spider onto another piece of paper behind the web, so that it can be seen when the door in the centre is opened.

MAKE A SNAIL

Provide self-hardening clay, plasticine or salt dough to make snails. Make a long thin strip to coil for the body and stumpy piece for the head and neck. Make indentations for eyes with a drinking straw or the end of a pencil. Use small pieces of raw spaghetti with a blob of modelling material on each for antennae.

FINGER MOUSE

1 Cut a strip of white or grey card. Roll loosely and tape or paste to make a cylinder.
2 Cut a quarter circle approx. 6cm radius. Tape to make a cone.
3 Cut circles for ears and paste onto the cone. Add eyes, whiskers, nose, etc with felt-tip pen. Paste a length of wool to the cylinder for a tail.
4 Join the two halves with a small strip of card. Bend this to form a hinge. The mouse puppet is operated by putting one finger into the cylinder.

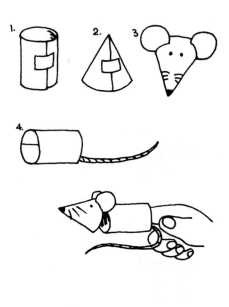

FLOWER POWER

Show a plant catalogue with varieties of plants named after famous people, eg roses. Encourage children to create and name their own flower by cutting a plastic drinking cup into strips from the top rim to the base, and fanning out the strips to form petals. Decorate the centre of the flower (the cup base) with screwed-up balls of brightly coloured paper. Flowers could be displayed together as a banner.

SAY IT WITH FLOWERS

You will need:
  Coloured card or stiff paper
  Florist's wire
  Pritt sticks or PVA glue and spreaders
  Half a potato and foil to cover it.

1 Draw round a template twice and cut out two flowers from bright coloured card or stiff paper. Older children may want to draw their own flower shapes.
2 In the centre of each flower write or draw something which reminds you of what Jesus has done for you. It could be a Bible verse, a song, a picture from a book, a symbol. (If you have labels you could write on those and stick them on.)
3 Bend the end of the wire. Put glue on the back of one of the flowers, lay the end of the wire in the centre and put the other flower on top of that.
4 Push the other end of the wire into half a potato covered in foil or into florist's block in a holder.

Alternatively use green pipe cleaners for stems and several circles of brightly coloured tissue paper for petals. Snip a small slit in the centre of the paper circles then push the pipe cleaner through and secure with sticky tape to make a flower.

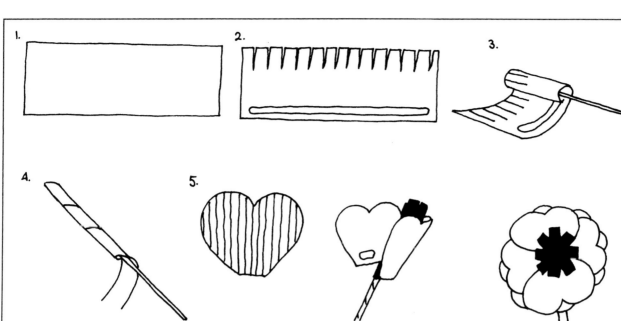

PAPER FLOWERS

This activity is suitable for older children. Follow the instructions to make paper flowers from crepe paper.

You will need:
Crepe paper
25cm lengths of garden wire
Black paper
Strong glue in a tube with a nozzle
Scissors

1 Cut out a piece of black paper about 5.5cm long and 2cm wide.
2 Make a fringe by cutting in from one of the long edges. Cut about halfway through.
3 Spread glue along the uncut edge and wind it onto the end of a piece of wire.
4 To cover the wire, spread glue on a long strip of green crepe paper and wind it down to the end.

5 Cut eight petals out of crepe paper. These should be roughly heart-shaped but with a squarer point. Cut them so that the crinkles on the crepe paper align as shown.
6 Shape the petals by stretching them a bit and then glue the bottom ends around the black centre.

SALT DOUGH PIGS

These instructions are for a flat pig, who will lie down or be a wall plaque with the child's or a recipient's name added! Make a model first, to show sizes of each part of the pig, but bear in mind that children's models are not meant to be identical.

You will need:
Paintbrushes
Water
Salt dough
Poster paints or watercolours from a child's paintbox
Polyurethane high gloss household varnish (for leader's use only)
Use basic quantity of salt dough recipe (see page 5, quantities given will make 8) and follow the instructions.
(This activity is quite fiddly and so most suitable for 8-10 year olds. It will need to be done over two sessions, to allow time for pigs to be baked.)

Divide the dough into eight roughly equal parts, one for each child. Each child needs to make:

→ a large oval for the body
→ a large circle for the head
→ a small circle for the nose
→ two triangles for ears
→ four short fat sausages for legs
→ a long thin sausage, curled, for the tail
→ a small heart (made either with a cutter or drawn onto the body with a cocktail stick)

1 Each child should use a paintbrush dipped in water to 'glue' the rest of the shapes onto the body.
2 The end of the paintbrush is used to make holes for eyes and nostrils.

3 Mark the child's initials on the back of each pig for identification.
4 Put pigs on an ovenproof tray and bake at 100°C/210° F/Gas Mark 1, for about 3 hours. Cooking time depends on the thickness of the models. Models are ready when the backs of the pigs are hard.
5 Bring the cooked models back to your group (can be done the following week) for the children to paint them.
When the paint is dry, an adult should apply varnish to the back of the pig first, then to the front. The varnish gives a rich shine and also preserves the dough.

7 Prayer

IT'S so easy to get into a rut about prayer, doing it mechanically or out of a sense of duty, or praying in the same way, week in week out. Sometimes this lack of creativity in prayer – for that's what it is – can spill over into our activities with young people, and quite unintentionally we convey to them the idea that prayer is difficult, boring, or an irksome duty. Yet if we can encourage children to pray we are giving them access to the most vital spiritual resource of all; they may not always have Bibles, songbooks, or other Christians but if they have learned to pray, they need never lose touch with God and his infinite resources.

Children are often much more spontaneous and creative in their praying than we are, and welcome unusual ways of praying. If the idea of prayers with a craft theme seems a bit strange, take a look at the activities in this section and be inspired to try some with your group!

CHRISTMAS PRAYER TREE

Make a Christmas tree from cardboard tubes wrapped cracker-style in green crepe paper and pasted on top of each other to make a pyramid. A small brown box at the base can serve as a trunk. You will need to include enough tubes to have one for each child. Write or draw a prayer or prayer-song on strips of Christmassy paper, roll up and place one inside each tube. At your prayer time each child untwists one end of a tube and removes and reads a prayer. A sticky label with the child's name can be attached to the end of the tube if you want to make the prayers more personal.

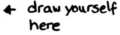

← fold on dotted lines

PRISM PRAYER CARDS

Follow instructions to make these simple stand-alone prayer cards.

• Cut the whole prayer card out. Colour in the text, draw yourself in the space provided and decorate around it.

• Fold along dotted lines and paste tab as shown.

← draw yourself here

34

COMPUTER PRAYER CARD

See illustration for design of card looking like a computer. Children should copy onto the 'screen' the following prayer, or paste on a photocopy, to be kept in their Bibles or by their beds. You could enlarge the design on a photocopier to make an A4 poster.

Lord, it would be nice if our lives worked like computers.
We'd like to **DELETE** the mistakes we make or things we don't enjoy.
We'd like to press the **SPACE BAR** to **FAST FORWARD** through hard times.
We'd like to **SAVE** happy times.
Help us to listen to your **INPUT**.
And may the **OUTPUT** of our mouths and lives be pleasing to you.
May we put your word in our **MEMORY**.
EXIT

WASHING LINE PRAYERS

Uses: *with themes on the family.*
Use pictures from magazines mounted on card, or let children draw pictures of their families or other people or things they are thankful for. Erect a low 'washing line' across the room or along a wall and encourage children to bring their pictures and to say a short 'thank you' prayer for that person or thing before pegging it on the line.

PAPER CHAIN PRAYERS

Uses: *with God's world or creation themes.*
Provide strips of coloured paper suitable for making into paper chains. Give each child two strips. On one they should write or draw something in God's world for which they want to say a special thank you; on the other they should write or draw something special about themselves to offer God. Build these up into a prayer chain using staples (quicker) or glue (fiddlier!), each child saying what (s)he has written as (s)he attaches them. Sum up with a thank you prayer.

HELICOPTERS

Make a copy of the helicopter illustrated for each child. Cut out around the outline and along the central line as far as the dotted line. Attach a paper clip to the tip. Fold down the flaps at the top in opposite directions. Hold folded end up and drop the helicopter from a good height (eg stand on a chair) and watch it whirl around as it descends. Each helicopter bears the caption, 'Don't whizz around all day; remember to stop, listen and pray.'

NB This is especially effective if the curved pattern appears on both sides of the helicopter because as it whirls to the ground a very effective optical illusion of a circle is created. However, it's difficult to reproduce this in a photocopiable resource book. You will therefore need to copy the curved pattern precisely onto the reverse side with a thick black marker before cutting the helicopter out if you would like to achieve this effect. If not, just reproduce the template outline without the pattern, and photocopy onto coloured paper.

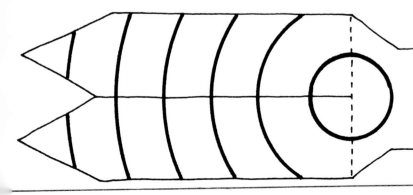

Don't whizz around all day; remember to stop, listen and pray.

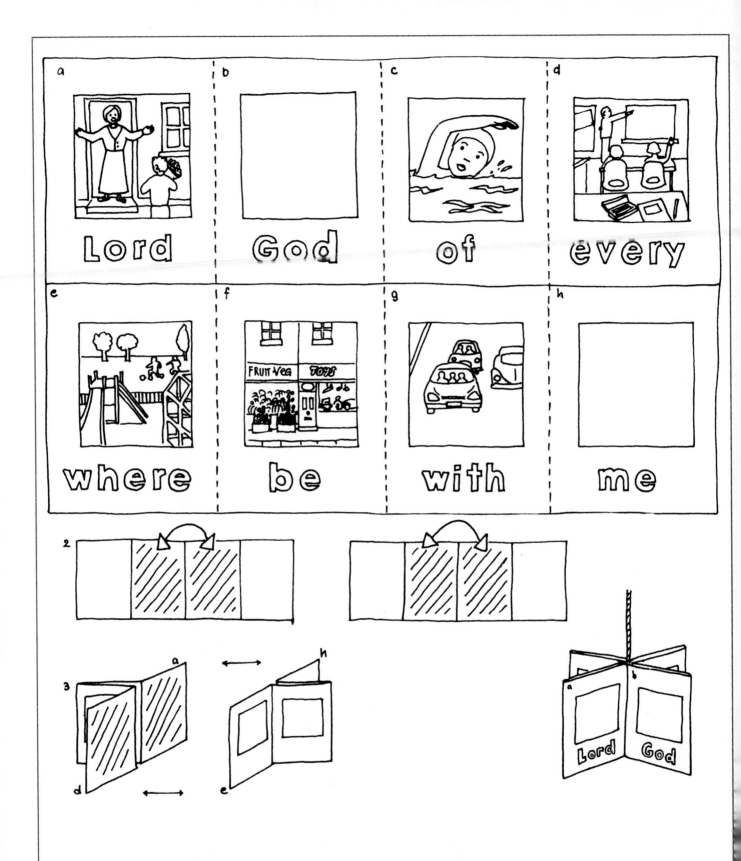

PRAYER MOBILE

Follow the instructions and illustrations given to make this particular mobile, or adapt it – using other pictures but the same method – as a craft resource for other prayer topics.

1 Cut illustration above into two strips. (Cut along solid lines, fold along broken lines.) Get children to colour pictures and words and draw their own pictures in b, and h.

2 Turn picture strips over. Paste the back of picture b to the back of picture c. Do the same with pictures f and g.

3 Paste the back of picture d to picture e. Place string or wool in the centre of the mobile and paste a to h.

PRAYER WHEEL

Uses: *Can be adapted for any 'thank you' topic.*
1 Cut out two 20cm/8 inch diameter circles for each child.
2 Divide one into three equal parts. Get the children to draw appropriate pictures in each section, eg for a creation theme: sky, plants or animals, people, etc.
3 Cut away one third of the second circle, write on a suitable caption or text, and fasten both wheels together with a 'split pin' or butterfly paper fastener. Turn top circle to change the pictures.

GRAFFITI WALL PRAYERS

Uses: *for the story of Nehemiah rebuilding the walls of Jerusalem, other building topics, or teaching about the church being made up of living stones.*

Using a strip of plain wallpaper or lining paper and a rectangular sponge dipped in pale brown paint, get the children to help paint a brick wall design. When dry, fix the paper to the wall at a height suitable for children to write on. Provide felt-tips or markers for children to write or draw prayer requests on the wall.

PAPER PLATE PRAYERS

Uses: *for Zacchaeus; adapt for other topics on change.*

Stick paper plates to sticks as in illustration. On one side in black write 'negative' words such as 'grabbing', 'hurting', 'unkind' and so on. On the reverse, in a brighter colour, write the opposite word such as 'giving', 'helping', 'kind'. Let children hold plates and turn them round as you say the following prayer: Lord, you changed Zacchaeus (or any other Bible character). Please change us... from **grabbing** to **giving**, from **hurting** to **helping**, etc. Amen.

FLYING MESSAGE (PAPER DART) PRAYERS

Uses: *for topics with a 'message' theme.*
Give each child a piece of A4 paper and a pen and ask them to write a prayer in response to what they have heard, for example thanking God that he speaks to us, or a prayer about something in the news. Then fold the messages into paper darts and let everyone aim them, at a given signal, into a bucket or an upturned umbrella.
1 Fold an A4 sheet of paper in half and open again.
2 Fold in the top corners.
3 Fold top corners over again.
4 Close sides together.
5 Fold out to make wings.

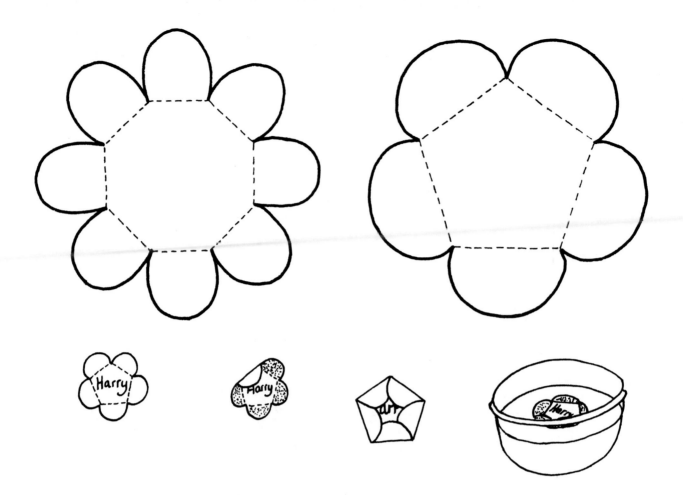

PRAYER FLOWERS

Uses: *for 'new life' themes or adapt for creation themes.*

Use the templates to make flowers which will open when put in water. Give each child a copy of the pattern on paper or thin card.

1 Cut out the shapes, colour in the petals and write in the centre of each flower the name of someone you would like to pray for.
2 Then fold the petals over, one at a time, along the dotted lines, working around the flower until the names are hidden. Fold them well but don't crease them with your thumbnail.
3 Tuck the corner of the last petal underneath the first one.
4 Drop the flowers (petal side up) carefully into a bowl of water so that they sit on the surface, and watch the petals open slowly.

ZIG-ZAG PRAYER BOOK

Make a zig-zag (concertina) book from large pieces of sugar paper. On each page put a picture, eg of food, animals, toys or clothes with a simple thank you prayer underneath. This could be used within the group, or children could make their own books by sticking in pre-cut pictures.

PEBBLE PRAYERS

Uses: *for themes where names are significant or when teaching about the church being made up of `living stones'.*

Have ready smooth, clean pebbles (or sugar paper in stone colours cut into pebble shapes) and felt-tip pens or thick gold and silver pens. Each child should choose a pebble and write his/her name on it. Put the pebbles together and let children pick one up and thank God for the person whose name is written there.

FLAG PRAYERS

Uses: *for Palm Sunday, praise, worship or celebration themes.*

Ask children to write short praise prayers on pieces of brightly coloured A4 paper (for Palm Sunday phrases such as 'Hosanna!' or `King Jesus!' or 'Welcome' would be appropriate). Secure a green garden stick along one side of each sheet to make a flag – a modern version of a palm branch.

Alternatively, cut out squares of paper, folded in half diagonally. Get children to write on one or both outer sides of the triangles, then fix them to a length of ribbon or coloured string by 'hanging' them along the fold and securing with staples to make bunting.

PRAYER BOUQUET

Give each child a card circle on which to write or draw a praise prayer, attach paper petals at the back and add a stem (pipe cleaner, green cane or drinking straw). Display all the prayers in a vase.

PRAYER KNOTS

Give each child a length of string. Ask them to tie a knot in the string for each member of their families. As they tie the knot they should think about the person, and what they find easy or difficult to relate to about him or her. Encourage them to pray to God, giving thanks for that person and asking for help over any difficulties in the relationship. The final knot should be much bigger and represents God. Encourage them to give thanks for what they know about God and ask for help with understanding the more difficult things. Finally tie the two ends of the string tightly together to make a circle representing God's relationship with us: his love never ends and he never stops remembering us even if we forget him.

PRAYER BOXES

Use the template and instructions to make a prayer box, in which children can place reminders of topics for prayer and perhaps a verse about prayer. These boxes can be decorated as you wish.

1 Photocopy (and enlarge) the templates on to thin card.
2 Cut along the thick black lines and fold along the dotted lines.
3 Stick down the tabs with glue.
4 Decorate the outside of the box.

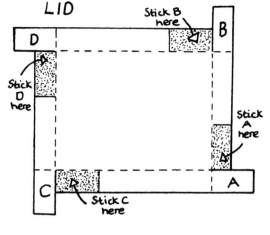

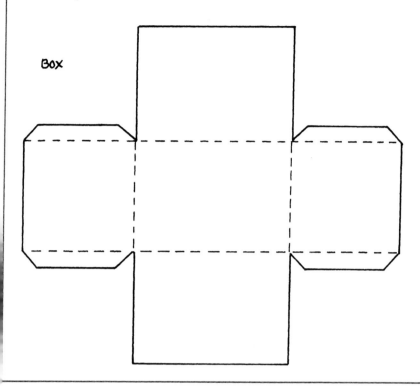

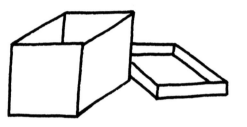

WINDMILL PRAYERS

Uses: *for topics to do with the Holy Spirit or wind.*

(The 'pattern' for these is found in Acts 4:23-31, where the believers, praying, first said something which focused on God's greatness and then asked for strength to do his work. Adapt this by suggesting that children first write something they know about God – 'Lord God, you...' and then ask for help for themselves or someone else.)

Write each part of the prayer on a square of coloured gummed paper (obviously lighter colours will show the words better), and stick these back to back. Alternatively, use special 'origami' paper which has a different colour on each side. Make them into a windmill as illustrated.

You will need:
    Large, headed pins (from the haberdashery department of a large store)
    Beads
    Corks
    Plant support canes

If using this activity in connection with the Holy Spirit, point out that as the windmills move when we blow on them, God sends the Holy Spirit to make the things that we have prayed for possible.

1 Push a cork on to the end of a garden stick.
2 Take the doublesided squares of coloured gummed paper (about 20cm square) and cut in about 10cm from each corner. (If you do this activity with younger children, you will need to do this beforehand.)
3 Fold alternate corners of the square to the centre and push a strong pin through them.
4 Pass the pin through the back of the windmill through a bead and into the cork.

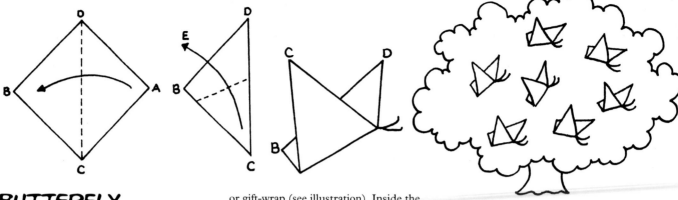

BUTTERFLY PRAYERS

Uses: *for God's world or for 'change' topics.*
Draw a bush appropriate to the size of your group (each child will be sticking a butterfly on it). Draw caterpillars on the bush. Make butterflies from a square of coloured paper or gift-wrap (see illustration). Inside the butterflies write the names of people who need Jesus' transforming power in their lives and hold the butterflies as you hold those people before God in prayer. Stick the butterflies onto the bush with a reminder the God does not always answer prayer in the way we expect. Write 'God changes caterpillars into butterflies. He changes people's lives too.' beside the bush.

1. Place paper coloured side down. Fold A to B along dotted line.
2. Fold C to E on dotted line.
3. Crease well. Draw feelers on background after sticking on.

PRAYER BUBBLES

Uses: *with topics on water.*
Mix thin paint with a generous squirt of washing up liquid, and pour into plastic cups and beakers to a depth of about 2cm. Blow (don't suck!) through a straw until the bubbles come up over the top of the container. Lower a plain piece of paper onto the bubbles and lift off carefully. Let children make one or two patterns and leave to dry. Whilst they are drying, use strips of paper to write simple prayers related to the day's theme, and stick these onto the bubble pictures when they are dry, pointing out that bubbles disappear very quickly, but God is always there, ready to listen to us. Mount the bubble prayers for an effective display, or, if children have had time to do more than one, let them take one home and display the other.

STICKING-PLASTER PRAYERS

Uses: *with topics on healing.*
Cut out and display newspaper headlines or photographs of situations (war, famine, refugees, disasters, etc) where people are hurting – physically or emotionally. Give each child a large piece of waterproof plaster dressing strip and a biro and ask them to write short prayers asking for God's healing in those situations, before sticking the plasters onto the headlines or photographs.

PRAYER BRICKS

Uses: *for topics about building, walls, or homes.*
Make a large drawing of a house with big, clearly defined bricks, or build a house front from boxes or large plastic bricks with labels stuck on them. Everyone writes or draws on a brick one thing about their home for which they want to thank God.

PRAYER CUBE

Use the template (copied onto sugar paper or thin card or stuck onto thin card) and let children cut round it to make a cube. Suggest that the children write or draw on each face of the cube something or someone they want to pray for/about. (Some children might like to label each face of the cube, in addition, with a day of the week, from Monday to Saturday, and use it as a daily prayer reminder, praying for all six topics on Sundays.) Practise folding templates into cubes before children start to paste! Assemble cubes by pasting on top of the tabs and sticking them under the matching sides. (The cube template can be adapted for other things, eg memory verses, photocubes with pictures of your church's mission partners or you could even leave the top unpasted and use it as a box.)

1. Draw and colour pictures and write words onto the squares.
2. Cut carefully all round the solid lines and fold down the dotted lines.
3. Fold your cross into a cube.
4. Paste the tops of tabs A, B and C and stick them under the matching sides.
5. Paste the tops of tabs D, E and F and stick them under the matching sides.
6. Finally paste tab G and slide under side G.

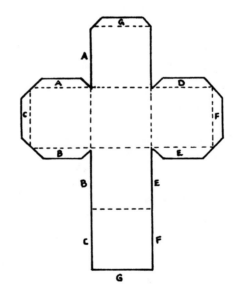

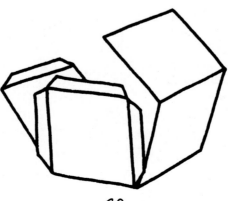

RAINBOW PRAYERS

Uses: *with topics on Noah, creation, water or colours.*
You will need:
Crepe paper in the seven rainbow colours
Newspapers
Roll newspaper into a thin tube and secure with sticky tape. Wind crepe paper in one colour round the newspaper tube to cover it. Attach at least two streamers of the same colour to the top of the tube. Teach a simple seven-word prayer such as 'Thank you God for loving us all'. Line children up holding their streamer-shakers in the order of the colours of the rainbow, then say the prayer slowly together, waving a different colour streamer for each word.

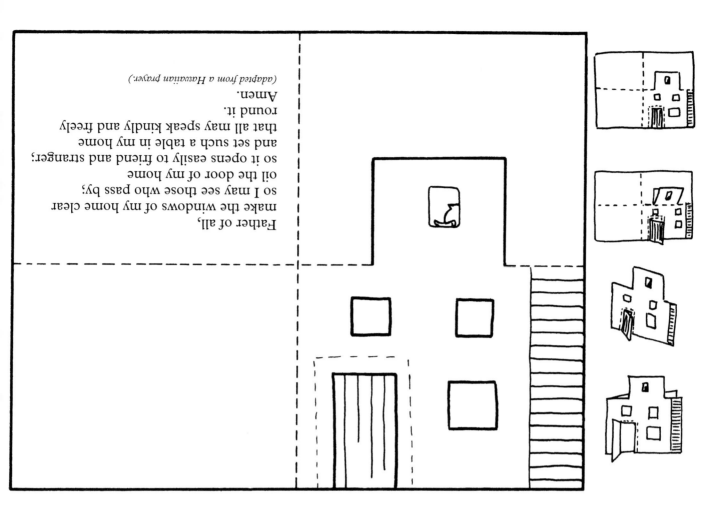

Father of all,
make the windows of my home clear
so I may see those who pass by;
oil the door of my home
so it opens easily to friend and stranger;
and set such a table in my home
that all may speak kindly and freely
round it.
Amen.

(adapted from a Hawaiian prayer.)

PRAYER HOUSE

Uses: *with the story of Elisha and the Shunemite woman who built him a guestroom, or in any discussion about sharing our homes with others.*

Photocopy the prayer house (preferably onto card) and make up according to the instructions. Point out the printed prayer.

1 Colour the house, including the room on the roof.
2 Cut along the solid black lines. (You may need to use a craft knife for the upper room and windows.)
3 Fold along the dotted lines.
4 Inside the door, draw a table and food.

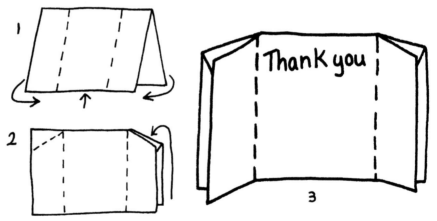

THANK YOU HOUSES

Uses: *for topics on homes or shelter.*
A quickie prayer activity! For preference, use coloured sheets of A4 paper which can be cut and folded to make a house-shaped card. The decoration can be as simple as just 'thank you' written inside, or they could be decorated with felt-tip pens, stickers, even straw for a thatched roof and so on.

1 Fold an A4 sheet of paper in half. Find centre and fold sides in.
2 Fold corners and tuck inside to make house shape.
3 Write 'Thank you' in centre and stand as shown.

5 Praise and celebration

CHRISTIANS have a lot to celebrate and joy should be one of the characteristics which mark us as Christians. Sometimes tiredness, stress and the 'cares of this life' as Jesus called them, weigh adults down; we don't feel like worshipping and praising God, and we need to be reminded of how great he is, and how worthy of our praise.

Children, by contrast, are usually very good at celebrating – another example of what it can mean to enter the kingdom of God with a childlike spirit. They love dressing-up (even if it's only a headband), singing, marching, making music and waving flags, balloons and banners. In fact, the instruction, 'Make a joyful noise to the Lord' could well have been designed for under-elevens! Let's channel their natural energy and exuberance into praising our great and wonderful Father God. There are just a few suggestions here but you will find ideas too in other sections, eg the sections devoted to festivals, 'party hats' in **Hats and headgear**, 'fish kites' in **Bible people** and 'paper lanterns' in **Bits and bobs**. Remember, it's possible to find something to celebrate in almost every topic!

LAUREL WREATHS

Explain that in Bible times a laurel wreath was a sign of honour and importance. Older children could be encouraged to write on each leaf something about Jesus, or a symbol such as a crown, a cross or a baby (because that is how he came to us). Make up the wreaths by photocopying onto thin card and cutting out the 'branches' shown here. Join them with sticky tape so that the wreath sits on the child's head. Alternatively make a simple cardboard headband and attach the laurel branches to it.

PASTA JEWELLERY

Thread holed pasta shapes onto cotton to make necklaces and headbands. Pasta can easily be coloured by dipping it in a concentrated solution of food colouring and leaving to dry overnight. An alternative to pasta is coloured plastic drinking straws, especially those in fluorescent colours, which look very attractive cut up and used as beads.

GARLANDS

Join about a metre of paper chain into a loop, or thread circles of crepe (or tissue) paper onto a piece of cotton.

LEAFY LULABS

These can be used to accompany singing, dancing or processions. Wind colourful ribbon around leafy branches. Metallic present ribbon, bows or the paper ribbon you can stretch and curl are very effective. Let children wave branches as they would have done in Bible times at the Festival of Shelters (see Leviticus 23:33-43).

Alternatively, make branches from 3 sheets of newspaper, tightly rolled, or use real twiggy branches, to which you attach strips of tissue or crepe paper in different colours. Make sure that branches do not have sharp points!

TOOTING TRUMPETS

Use quarter circles of clean stiff card, and glue on any shiny materials suitable for decorating them. When decorating is complete, roll into a trumpet shape and tape in place (see illustration). Attach streamers to the bottom of the trumpet to decorate.

ANGEL BAND

See illustration on next page for ideas for making instruments from shiny Junk': gold and silver foil scraps; foil containers; shoe boxes; pasta shapes sprayed gold and silver; cardboard tubes, etc.

Although this was originally a Christmas activity, it can obviously be used for other celebrations too.

Trumpets
Cover a cardboard tube and a plastic cup in foil. Tape the cup onto the end of the tube and attach gold and silver shreds to decorate.

Shakers
a. Fill a clear plastic drinks bottle with pasta shapes, etc sprayed gold and silver.
b. Tape foil containers together with rice, or similar material inside, and decorate with tinsel shreds.

Rainsticks
Cover a cardboard tube in foil and place rice or dried peas inside. Cover the ends and decorate with gold bands and sequins.

Harps
Cover a shoe box in foil and wrap elastic bands around it as shown. Decorate with tinsel or streamers.

Other instrument ideas include:

Plate shaker
Staple two paper plates together with some dry rice in the middle.

Cup shaker
Tape two paper cups together with dry rice or beans inside.

String shakers
Make a necklace of clean foil bottletops or crisp packets. Rustle and shake.

Drum
Fix a piece of paper over a paper cup with a strong elastic band; tap with fingers.

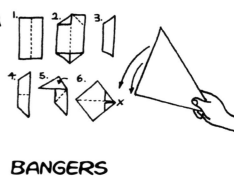

BANGERS

This activity gives a new twist to the instruction "Make a joyful noise"! It's probably not suitable for very young children who don't like bangs. Practise beforehand if you want to use them in a special service.

1 Fold a large sheet of newspaper down the centre. (NB It must be newspaper. Ordinary paper is too thick and inflexible for this to work.)
2 Open again and fold the corners to the centre line.
3 Fold together again.
4 Fold in half, top to bottom, then unfold again.
5 Fold the points over to the centre line.
6 Turn the whole shape over and fold it back on itself.
7 To make a big BANG! hold the tip (x) and jerk down sharply.

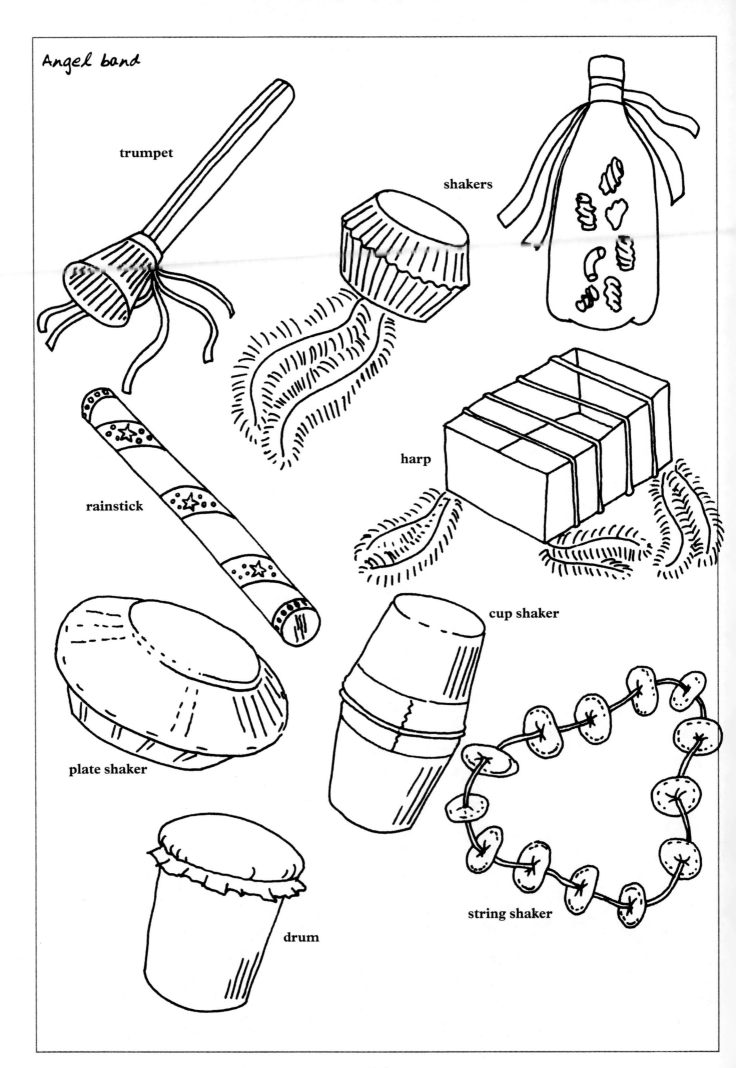

Angel band

trumpet

shakers

rainstick

harp

plate shaker

cup shaker

drum

string shaker

9 Bible people

THE Bible is not just a theoretical holy book: rather it is a record of God acting in the world and in history. Many parts of the Bible, especially the Old Testament, the Gospels and Acts, tell of God's dealings with people, in particular with his special people, first the Israelites and then the church. We sometimes tend to put these Bible people on a pedestal, but if we read the Bible closely we shall find that they were – like us – only too human. The Bible shows us God's people 'warts and all', and that should encourage us, because the God who didn't give up on devious Jacob and who found the adulterer and murderer King David 'a man after his own heart' is the God who is ever ready to welcome and forgive us.

In this section you will find a number of activities linked to specific Bible stories and characters, but even if the one you want isn't here, you may find you can adapt an activity to `fit' another character or story – perhaps with the help of one of the puppet or model ideas (see **Introduction**).

NEHEMIAH (rebuilding the walls of Jerusalem)

BUILD A PRAYER-WALL!

→ **Under fives:** give each child a large brick made of a taped up cereal box — the children could paint or decorate these beforehand if there is time. Ask the children one by one what they want to talk to God about or say thank you for, and as you pray for that, let the child bring the brick forward to make the wall.

→ **5+:** Graffiti wall – give children pieces of rectangular sponge and light brown paint and let them paint a brick design on a large piece of lining or wallpaper. Allow it to dry, then fix it to the real wall at a height at which the children can write on their prayer requests.

BRICK-MAKING

This can be quite a messy activity so make sure you have covered work surfaces and clothes before you start.

Mix plaster of Paris to the consistency of double cream. Soak small rectangles of sponge into the mixture, squeeze and release until the plaster of Paris is absorbed. Lift out carefully and leave to dry for about 20-30 minutes on a piece of paper, by which time the 'bricks' should be hard enough to be painted or decorated with felt tips.

NOAH

In addition to activities outlined below see also 'Rainbows' in section on **Weather**, `Ravens' in **God's world** and 'Doves' in **Pentecost**.

SEASONS CIRCULAR

Follow the directions to make revolving paper shapes representing the four seasons. Colour each section brightly with colours appropriate to that season and carry them in procession singing seasonal songs appropriate to your area.

Cut two identical squares of stiff paper (approximately 20-30cm square). Fold top corners as indicated. Cut slits, then slot the two cards together at right angles, securing with sticky tape if they tend to go flat. Attach a string to the centre.

Colour each section to represent one of the four seasons. Hold by the string and walk: the 'seasons circular' will rotate. The faster you walk, the faster it will rotate.

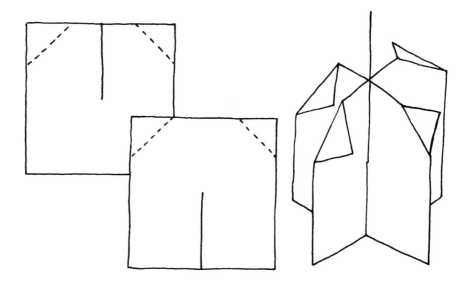

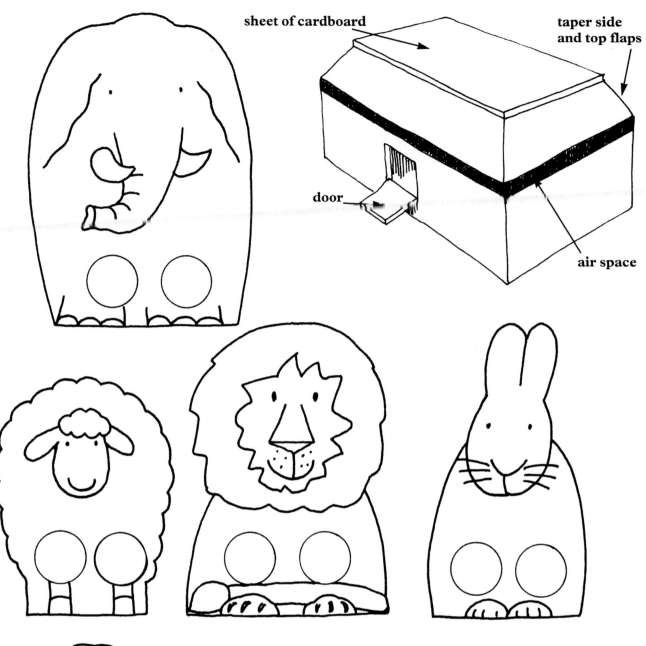

sheet of cardboard

taper side and top flaps

door

air space

MODEL ARK AND WALKING ANIMAL PUPPETS

Make an ark from a large cardboard grocery box as shown and use in conjunction with pairs of animal puppets – see illustration.

The ark

1 Use a long cardboard box with flaps.
2 Taper side and top flaps to meet, and form roof using sticky tape. Lay a removable sheet of cardboard on top to complete roof.
3 On one side of the box, cut the top and two sides of the door, folding down the fourth side to make ramp.
4 Shade in an air space.

Walking animal puppets

1 Photocopy or draw templates onto stiff paper or thin card and cut out.
2 Cut out the 'finger holes' (large enough for the children's fingers to go through and bend over).

46

THE LAME MAN at the pool of Bethesda

JOINTED PUPPET (A)

Use one of the templates for a jointed puppet. The one joined only with paper-fasteners is simpler for younger children, but the jumping one is more dramatic! If you want to use the jumping one with under-sevens, you will need to do the actual assembly yourself after children have coloured the parts, so it's not really practical with anything but a small group of young children.

Make the sick man well:

1 Photocopy or mount the parts for Puppet A onto card.
2 Cut them out and colour in.
3 Put them together with paper fasteners where marked, making sure that the arms and legs move freely. Make the man dance to show that he is well and happy.

JUMPING PUPPET (B)

Follow the steps above with the slightly more complicated parts for Puppet B.

On the back, join the tops of the arms together at point 'y' with a short loose thread. Join the tops of the legs together in the same way.

Tie the two short lengths of thread together with a long thread, which hangs down below the puppet.

Attach a loop of thread to the top of the head. Pull the long thread and the person jumps.

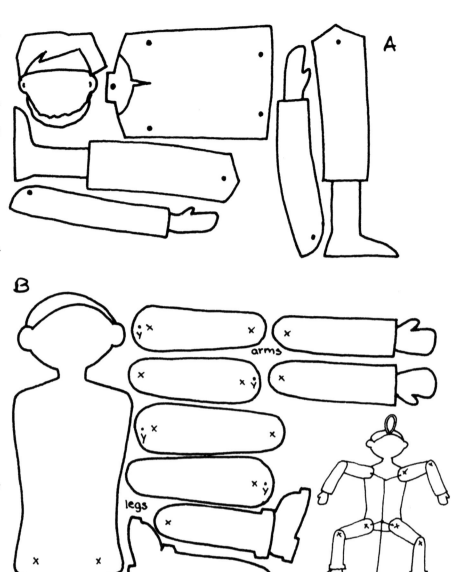

ZACCHAEUS

ZACCHAEUS IN THE TREE

Note: This is a fairly simple activity, but try it beforehand to get the proportions right. For each child cut out a tree trunk shape from brown card and a green tree-foliage shape. (Alternatively you could decorate the tree with a collage of scrunched up green tissue.) Fold the green shape down the centre and tape or glue it (as shown in illustration) on to the side edges only of the trunk shape. Cut out and colour a Zacchaeus figure. Fix a strip of card a little wider than Zacchaeus to the back of the trunk, near the top. Attach Zacchaeus to a drinking straw or strip of firm card and slot it through the card strip on the tree trunk. The figure can then be lowered or raised as required in retelling the story.

BEFORE AND AFTER FRIEZE

Make a 'before and after' picture of the Zacchaeus story to draw out the change in Zacchaeus.

1 Using a strip of decorator's lining paper as a background, draw lines on for the road, as shown.

2 Build up *the back view* only of the crowd by cutting out and pasting on triangles, circles and other shapes cut from wrapping paper scraps. Use large triangles for bodies, small ones for arms and circles for heads. Make the tree from brown and green magazine scraps.

3 Complete the frieze by placing Zacchaeus in the tree and build up the front view of the crowd, giving these people smiley faces – only Jesus could bring about a change like that.

JERICHO SQUARE

Photocopy the illustration below onto thick paper or thin card for each child. Explain that there are lots of people in the tree because we are all like Zacchaeus and do wrong things (some of which could be written on the tree). Children should colour in the scene and add their own names in the space at the bottom. Complete the model by cutting along the thick black lines and folding along dotted lines. (A small cut by an adult with a craft knife around the tree will help them get started with the scissors.) Stick the shaded strip at the top, to the base.

See also **Prayer** section (Paper plate prayers') for a link with Zacchaeus.

Stick this strip down

Jesus says 'Hurry down .... because
I must stay in your house today.

Matthew

Jesus

MATTHEW & JESUS HAND PUPPETS

Although these are specifically designed as either visual aids or craft activities for the story of how Jesus met Matthew, the idea –and the faces illustrated – can be adapted for use with other Bible characters.

1 Choose two contrasting tea towels or large scraps of cloth – an old shirt or T-shirt for example.
2 Clenching your fist, place one over your hand and slip a rubber band loosely around your wrist to form the puppet's head. Pull your hand out, leaving the rubber band in position. (This makes putting on the puppet easy next time.)
3 Draw or photocopy two faces onto paper and cut out. These can be glued, taped or sewn into place.

JOSEPH, MARY AND ANGEL FINGER PUPPETS

To make the finger puppets, photocopy the illustration on to strong paper, cut out the figures, cut on dotted lines under arms, and tape to make into cylinders to fit round fingers.

JESUS AND TEN LEPERS

JESUS AND TEN LEPERS CYLINDER PUPPETS

Like other puppets in this section, the method shown here can be used for other characters.

From a piece of paper (about A5), cut out the shape of a head and arms as shown. (Cut away the shaded area). Colour or decorate the remaining piece, adding features. Roll the lower half into a cylinder and tape at the back. Make ten puppets plus one to represent Jesus.

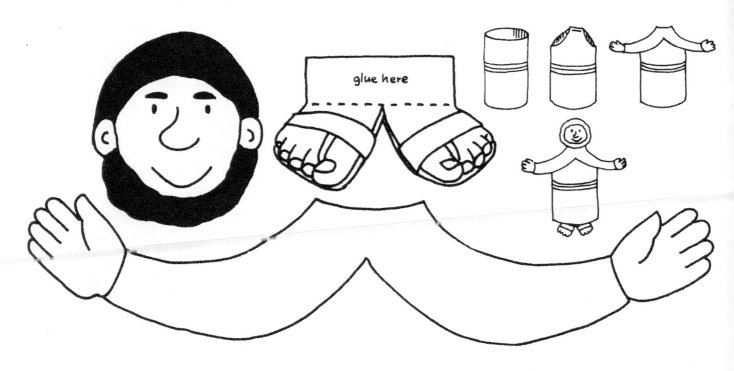

PAUL

PAUL PREACHING MODEL

This model could also be used for any of the apostles or any preaching story.

1 Glue paper or material onto a toilet roll or half a kitchen roll tube and decorate as a body.
2 Pinch the top and cut off the 'corners'. Staple top together.
3 Use the pattern given (actual size) to make arms, feet and a head, and glue or staple the arms on before adding the head. Attach feet by gluing tab inside the tube.

PAUL AND BARNABAS 'WALKING MODELS'

Copy or photocopy the figures of the apostles onto strong paper or thin card and let children colour, collage or decorate them. Cut out finger holes (a craft knife is best for this, but should be used only by an adult or with careful adult supervision). Put fingers through holes from back to make two 'walking' models.

PAUL AND BARNABAS MATCHBOX PUPPETS

Use matchbox 'sleeves', one for each child. Cover each side of the sleeve with a piece of plain paper (or a sticky address label) and let children draw faces on them. Show them how to cover two fingers with a scrap of material before putting the matchbox sleeve on top to make a simple puppet.

Adapt this for other characters, especially if you want to show a change in somebody – a different expression on the front and back of the matchbox sleeve.

SOLDIERS

PEG DOLL SOLDIERS

Soldiers feature in many Bible stories – the OT kings frequently had armies, the Gospels tell the story of Jesus played out against a background of a land occupied by Roman soldiers, and Paul often uses soldier images in his letters. This particular activity is simple enough for the youngest children to enjoy, but could be done by older ones independently and quickly, maybe as a group activity, where a number of soldiers are needed, perhaps for a model.

To make these model soldiers you will need to get hold of old-fashioned wooden clothes pegs.

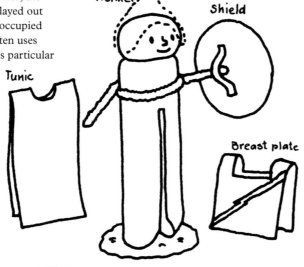

You can dress the soldier in whatever scraps of material or crepe paper you have available but you will need pipe-cleaners for arms, aluminium foil to make a helmet and breastplate and an oval of card for a shield. Stand the finished soldier in plasticine or playdough.

Helmet
Mould a piece of aluminium foil round the head in the shape of a helmet.

Tunic
Fold length of red crepe paper in half. Cut a hole for the head and tie tunic around the waist to secure it.

Shields
Cut an oval of card and tape a loop on the back.

Breastplate
Cut a generous length of foil. Fold in half and cut as shown. Place over the head and mould the foil together at the sides.

SHIELDS

For younger children: help them decorate shield shaped pieces of cardboard cut from grocery cartons. Tape two loops of string to the back of each shield for easier holding. Write on the front of each shield an appropriate statement such as 'Jesus is alive', and let children march with them.

FISHERMEN

FISH KITES

The Gospels have many `fishing' stories, since several of the disciples were fishermen by trade. Here is a slightly different fish activity.

You will need:
 Lightweight paper and things to decorate it with
 Flower wire
 Sticky tape
 Garden canes
 String

1 Enlarge the fish outline several times (to approximately 50cm in length)
2 Cut out two fish shapes from lightweight paper and colour both sides or paste on paper shapes.
3 Paste the two fish together along the top and bottom – make sure the hole at the mouth is larger than the hole at the tail so that the fish inflates in the wind.
4 Fold the mouth flaps inwards over a circle of wire and secure with sticky tape. (Thin flower wire used double is easy to handle.)
5 Attach a short piece of string to the wire at either side of the mouth and attach a stick or washing line.

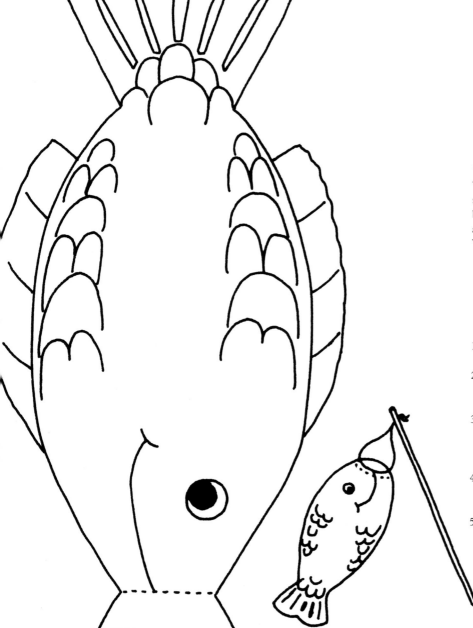

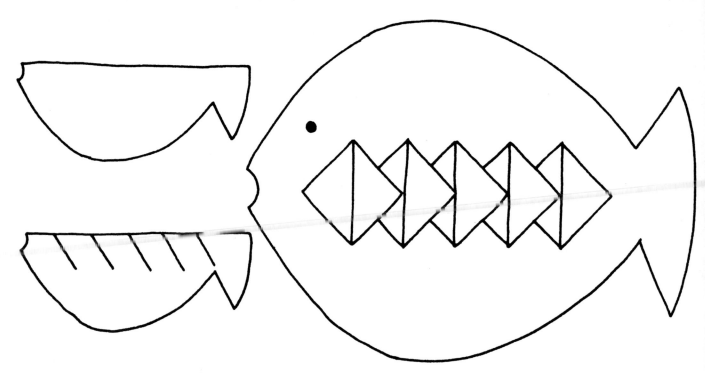

'WE WILL FOLLOW' POSTER OR CARD

You will need:

Strong, coloured paper (for a special occasion origami paper, which is a different colour on each side, would be particularly effective)
Scissors
Glue
Background sheet of paper in a contrasting colour

1 Cut out a simple fish shape.
2 Fold in half and make angled cuts: longer in the middle, shorter at the outside.
3 Fold back each V shape.
4 Write the child's name on the tail.
5 Paste fishes onto background with heading 'Jesus we will follow you'.

ELISHA

EASTERN HOUSE COLLAGE

You will need:

Squares of polystyrene (packing tiles)
Black squares of paper or material for doors and windows
Pre-cut zigzags of polystyrene for stairs
A large piece of dark card for a background

Make individual houses, then group them together to look like an Eastern town. (The guestroom on the roof is the clue that this was originally devised to go with the Elisha story, but it could be used for any Bible town collage, eg Bethlehem for Christmas stories. You could simplify the making for younger children by leaving off the guestroom, and the house sizes could be varied.)

For each house

1 Use two squares of polystyrene tile, one smaller than the other. Cut each into quarters. Use one quarter of each tile for the lower and upper rooms.
2 Cut another large tile into quarters. Cut each quarter to make two staircases as shown. This will give you 8 sets of steps from one tile.
3 Cut black paper doors and windows.
4 Assemble house on large piece of card, using PVA adhesive.

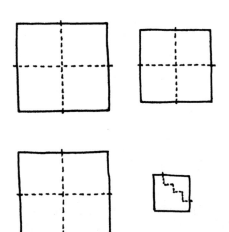

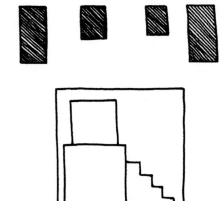

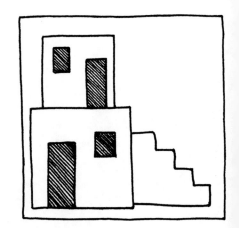

ALL HE NEEDS

This is a very simple craft activity which can be used to retell the story of Elisha's guestroom. Give each child four narrow strips of card and three 'split pin' fasteners, and show them how to make a house, bed, table and chair.

(See also 'Prayer house' in **Prayers** section.)

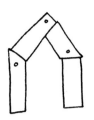
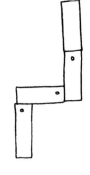

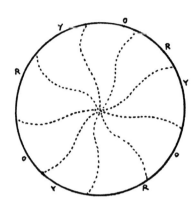

MOSES

BURNING BUSH CARD

The finished card looks very effective, but if you want to do this with younger children, it would be a good idea to do all the cutting out beforehand with a craft knife. Older groups with plenty of time might like to use torn pieces of yellow, red and orange tissue paper, instead of crayons to colour the wheel.

1 Enlarge the illustration. Cut out and colour the flame wheel in bright flame

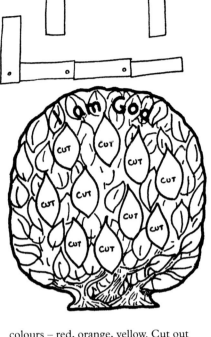

colours – red, orange, yellow. Cut out and colour the bush in brown and green/yellow. Write 'I am God' on the top of the bush.

2 Cut out the flame shapes from the bush. Push a paper fastener (split pin) through the centre dot on the bush, then through the centre of the wheel. Open the 'arms' of the paper fastener and press flat.

3 Turn the wheel and watch the flames flicker in the bush.

ELIJAH

See also 'Ravens' activities in **Birds**.

NICODEMUS

See windmill and kite activities for 'wind' in **Pentecost** section.

THE SAMARITAN WOMAN AT THE WELL

See ideas for water collages and streamers in **Weather** section.

Also, make thumb or coil pots from clay which doesn't need firing.

THOMAS

See 'Swizzlesticks' activity in **Easter** section.

MARTHA AND MARY

SAD AND HAPPY FACES

Use in connection with the death of Lazarus. Photocopy the figures of Mary and Martha (below) and paste them onto thin card, Cut them out and colour them in. Attach the faces with a butterfly clip in the centre and turn them round to reveal either a happy or sad expression.

10 Angels

MENTION the word 'angels' to anyone working with young people in a church and they will immediately think 'Christmas'. Of course angels do feature several times in the stories we hear and tell every Christmas and Advent: Gabriel's appearance to Zechariah in the temple; his visit to Mary; the message of reassurance for Joseph; the 'heavenly host' who gave the good news to the shepherds; the angel's warning to Joseph to take Mary and Jesus into Egypt, so it's not surprising that the two are inextricably linked in our minds and you will find here several traditional Christmas craft activities involving angels.

However, angels also feature in many other stories in both Old and New Testament, from the Garden of Eden, through Abraham, Jacob, the Exodus, Samson, Gideon, Elijah, Daniel and the Prophets, to mention but a few, and then we find them mentioned also in the Gospels, Acts and Revelation. So there may well be other times when you can use an angel activity and many of these ideas can easily be adapted for non-Christmas themes.

ANGEL CARDS

Using the illustration provided and a craft knife, cut your own templates from thick card or from the lids of ice-cream cartons. These are ideal because they are white (so can be drawn on easily), easy to cut, and washable. **NB** If you cut carefully with a craft knife, the 'hole' left after making the template can be used as a stencil (see below). Provide ready folded card to make individual cards, and show children how to draw round the template and paint in bright colours (who says angels have to be white and gold?) and then add glitter, etc if desired.

ANGEL STENCIL

1 Place the stencil onto a piece of coloured paper or card. (Young children may have to be shown how to use a stencil and under-fives will benefit from having it anchored to the background with small blobs of *Blu-tack*.)

2 Holding the angel outline stencil firmly with one hand, paint across the outline and the card, using gold, silver or white paint.

3 Remove the stencil to see your coloured angel.

ANGEL MESSAGE

(older children)

This activity is suitable for any topic which involves an angel bringing a message – which includes most of the most popular stories about angels in the Bible! Part of the angel's message is copied onto the angel as a reminder that God always keeps his word.

Copy the angel template onto thin card (this is one activity where card is essential as the finished angel has to stand up), and provide three for each child. They will also need paste, scissors, glitter and if possible gold or silver pens to write on the models. Demonstrate how to draw round and cut out three angel figures and fold each one exactly down the centre. (Do this in advance for less co-ordinated children or if you are short of time.) The angels will not stand up if they are not cut carefully. Invite the children to suggest a suitable phrase or sentence from the angel's message to write on the finished model, and then decorate with glitter after writing on the message. NB Decorate and write on the angels *before* trying to stick them together!

Demonstrate how to put paste on the back of *half* an angel (B), and press that half carefully onto the half-back of another (C), making sure the bottom edges are level. Now put paste across the whole back of the third angel (A,D) and press it onto the unpasted two half-backs of the other angels (E,F), again lining up the bottom edges. The angels should stand up (but you may need to wait for the paste to dry before they do).

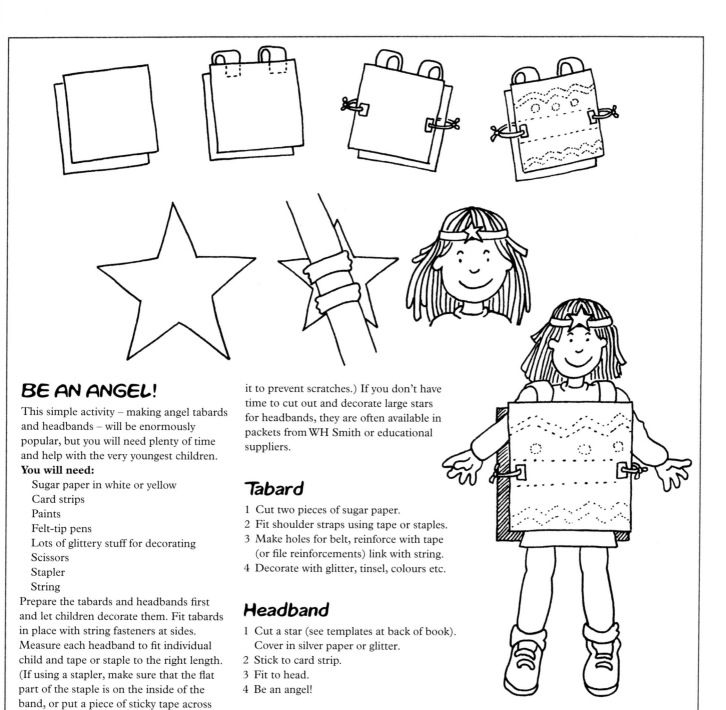

BE AN ANGEL!

This simple activity – making angel tabards and headbands – will be enormously popular, but you will need plenty of time and help with the very youngest children.

You will need:

    Sugar paper in white or yellow
    Card strips
    Paints
    Felt-tip pens
    Lots of glittery stuff for decorating
    Scissors
    Stapler
    String

Prepare the tabards and headbands first and let children decorate them. Fit tabards in place with string fasteners at sides. Measure each headband to fit individual child and tape or staple to the right length. (If using a stapler, make sure that the flat part of the staple is on the inside of the band, or put a piece of sticky tape across it to prevent scratches.) If you don't have time to cut out and decorate large stars for headbands, they are often available in packets from WH Smith or educational suppliers.

Tabard

1 Cut two pieces of sugar paper.
2 Fit shoulder straps using tape or staples.
3 Make holes for belt, reinforce with tape (or file reinforcements) link with string.
4 Decorate with glitter, tinsel, colours etc.

Headband

1 Cut a star (see templates at back of book). Cover in silver paper or glitter.
2 Stick to card strip.
3 Fit to head.
4 Be an angel!

POP-UP ANGEL CARD

This card can be decorated as simply or elaborately as you wish.

1 Fold an A5 sheet of card or stiff paper.
2 Decorate it and write a Christmas message on the front.
3 Cut out and colour in an angel shape.
4 Fold the tabs under. Open the card and paste the tabs 2cm from the centre fold on each side.
5 Check carefully that the angel folds in the correct place.

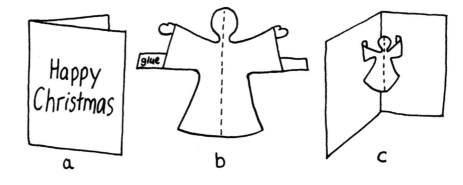

a   b   c

ANGEL CRACKERS

You will need:
Crepe paper
Tinsel
Cut kitchen roll tubes
Wrapped chocolates or similar
Foil outlines of angels

1 Cut a length of cardboard tube and pack it with sweets or other gifts.
2 Cut a piece of crepe paper twice the length of the tube and wrap it around the tube.
3 Tie tinsel to close the ends.
4 Glue an angel outline cut from foil (or shiny/foil-backed card) to the cracker.

SHINING ANGELS

(for younger children)
Use any simple angel template (see back of book) and provide several sizes of angel cut-outs in white paper. Let children decorate their angels as they wish, using glitter, foil, sticker stars, tinsel, doilies, tissue paper, coloured cellophane, etc. Mount on dark, background paper.

POP-UP ANGEL I

For each angel you will need:
A paper doily
A plastic bottle and piece of dowelling
A large sticky label (optional)
Card
Strands of wool
Paste
Scissors and decorative wrapping paper, eg Christmas paper
Also, all the usual glittery bits and pieces essential for angel-making!

(Make a hole in the base of the bottle in advance, eg with a hot knitting needle or skewer, and cut the top from the bottle to leave a depth of about 15cm. If the top is rough, sand it down.)

1 Cut the doily in half. Make one part into a cone and paste to the top of the dowel.
2 Cut a circle from the card and draw a face onto it, using wool for hair.
3 Attach head to body.
4 Make wings from the other half of the doily and attach them so that they do not stick out too far.
5 Cover the bottle with wrapping paper and, if you wish, write a suitable caption relating to the Bible story, on a large sticky label and stick it on the bottle.
6 Push the dowel through the hole so that the angel pops up and down.

POP-UP ANGEL 2

A slightly different pop-up angel intended to be used as a toy by younger children.

You will need:

  A clean plastic drinks bottle
  Wrapping paper
  PVA glue
  Sticky tape
  Card
  Dowelling rods or garden canes
  Foil
  Tinsel
  Glitter
  Doilies

1 Before the session, cut top off bottle (sand cut edges if necessary) and make a hole in the bottom.

2 Cut a card angel shape (slightly shorter than the depth of the cut off bottle so that when the angel is not popping up, it's hidden inside the bottle).

3 Decorate angel with foil, glitter, tinsel, etc.

4 Decorate bottle with wrapping paper, glitter, etc.

5 Tape dowel (or plant support cane) to back of angel.

6 Push dowel into bottle (from top) and through hole.

7 Pop-up an angel!

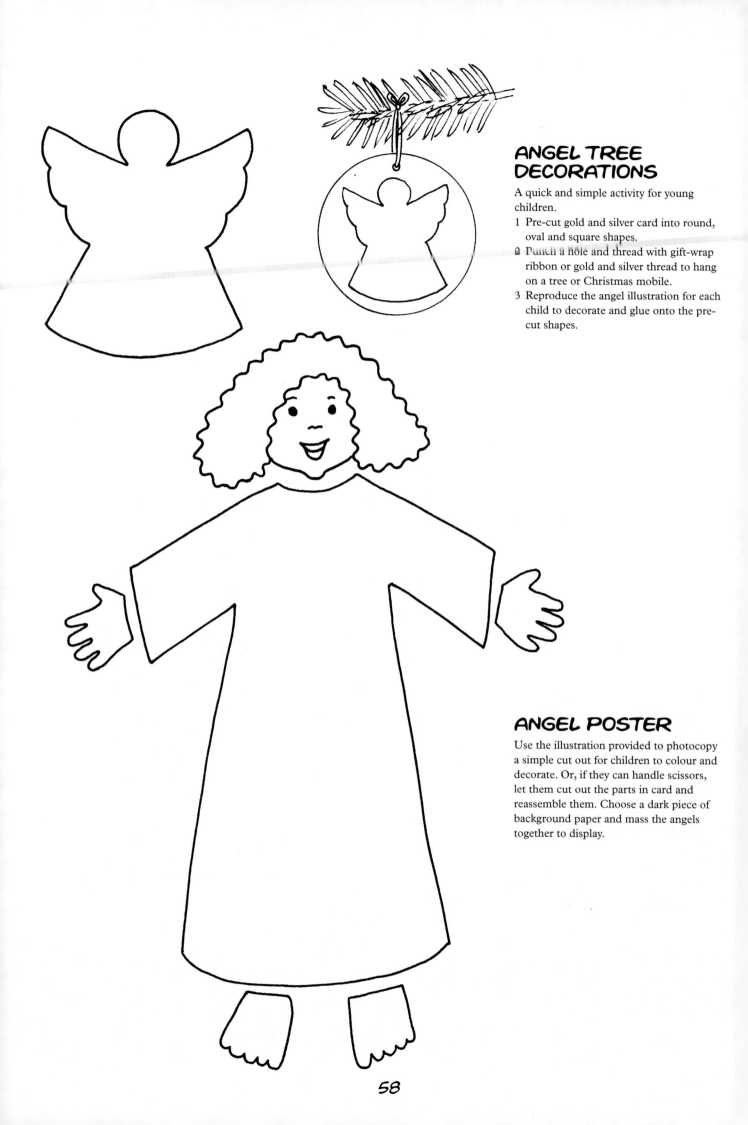

ANGEL TREE DECORATIONS

A quick and simple activity for young children.

1 Pre-cut gold and silver card into round, oval and square shapes.
2 Punch a hole and thread with gift-wrap ribbon or gold and silver thread to hang on a tree or Christmas mobile.
3 Reproduce the angel illustration for each child to decorate and glue onto the pre-cut shapes.

ANGEL POSTER

Use the illustration provided to photocopy a simple cut out for children to colour and decorate. Or, if they can handle scissors, let them cut out the parts in card and reassemble them. Choose a dark piece of background paper and mass the angels together to display.

3-D ANGEL PICTURES

Use the illustration provided. Give each child three copies to colour, then follow the assembly instructions.

1 Paste one onto a rectangle of thick card.
2 Stick the other two on top using 'sticky-fixer' pads – one on top of the other. (You could also use little squares of thick corrugated cardboard.)
3 Print the following verse below the angel: We know that Jesus really is the Saviour of the world. (John 4:42)
4 Fix a ribbon loop on to the back for hanging up.

See also:

- **Bible people** section for 'Angel finger puppet'
- **Praise & celebration** section for 'Angel band'

We know that Jesus really is the Saviour of the world. John 4:42

11 Weather

THE British notice the weather – it's an endless source of fascination simply because, as someone once put it, 'we get so much of it' and its very unpredictability gives it added interest. The climate of Bible lands being Mediterranean rather than temperate, the Bible, especially the book of Psalms, has more references to drought and the desirability of rain and protection from the sun than it might have done had it been set in Britain.

Most of the Biblical narrative concerns people who were almost entirely dependent on the land for their livelihood, so were affected by the weather much more than we are today in an urban and industrial society. Many stories in the Bible therefore have a weather element – too much rain, as in the story of Noah, or not enough, as in several drought stories, notably Elijah on Mount Carmel – whilst Jesus' own weather knowledge is seen in parables, and in his references to looking at the sky and predicting the weather (see Mark 4:1-20 and Matthew 16:1-3 respectively).

Our craft activities focus on God's control over the weather, and the changing seasons ('seedtime and harvest'), in relation to his provision. The activities below link with those in **God's world**, with some in **Prayer**, with wind ideas in **Pentecost**, and see also 'Seasons Circular' in **Bible people**.

MAKE A RAINBOW

Prepare seven 'arches' of paper or thin card that will fit together to form a rainbow. Divide children into small groups and give each an arch to fill in, using materials of an appropriate colour. From largest to smallest (or outer to inner) arch you will need red, orange, yellow, green, blue, indigo, violet. Materials can be anything from felt-tip pens to torn-up magazine pictures or crepe and tissue paper. When you display the finished rainbow, put a verse appropriate to the topic in the semicircle at the base.

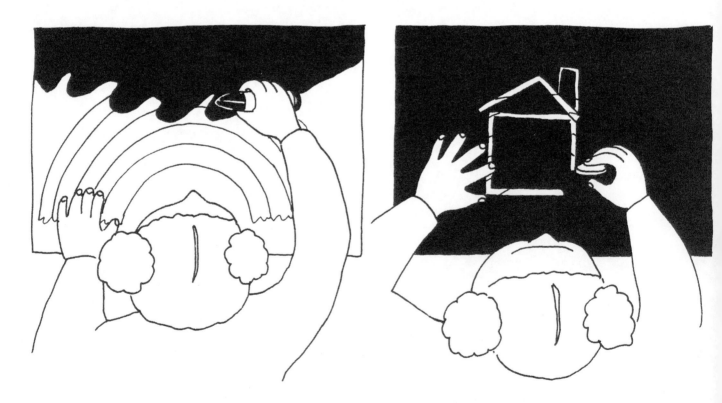

WAX RESIST RAINBOW PICTURES

You will need:
   Wax crayons in rainbow colours
   Black, thick paper (about A5 size)
   Coins for rubbing
Younger children would probably benefit from a rainbow outline drawn on the paper beforehand but children aged 5 and upwards will probably happily draw one themselves.

Encourage children to colour broad arcs of rainbow colours to fill the paper, and then colour with black wax crayon over what they have done. Show them how to sweep with a coin over the black wax to reveal the rainbow underneath.

SPECTRUM SPINNERS

(age 7 upwards)

Uses: *for topics on weather, colour, creation or even the wonders of eyesight.*

You will need:

- Crayons
- Short pencils (for spinning)
- Plasticine
- White card
- Protractor

Beforehand: divide small circles of white card (the backs of old greeting cards work well for this), into 7 equal sections. This is not easy since 360° doesn't divide exactly by 7!) so use a protractor to make an angle of 51° at the base of 4 sections, and of 52° at the base of the other three.

Explain how a rainbow is formed when light shines through raindrops, which breaks the light up into the colours of the spectrum, or the 'rainbow' colours. Let children make a hole in the centre of the card by pushing the pencil point through into some plasticine. Remove pencil while children colour the 7 sections of the card in the 7 rainbow colours. Put the pencil into the hole, point downwards, and spin the card circles. Watch the colours disappear! Explain that when the circle spins very fast, our eyes can't distinguish the different sections and the colours join together to make white.

A variation on this is to put dots all over the circles in red, yellow and blue (the primary colours) and spin as above. The dots will become lines of colour, and merge to produce different shades.

WATERFALL COLLAGE

Make a collage waterfall using bubble wrap, shiny blue/green paper and cellophane, crepe and tissue paper.

To use with the story of the Samaritan woman at the well, make two waterfalls, labelling one, 'Why do we need water?' and the other 'Why do we need Jesus?' Paste on responses as children suggest ideas.

STREAMERS

Make streamers using the sorts of paper suggested for the waterfall collage (above), and attach to garden support canes. You could also attach strips of paper with the sort of responses suggested in the Waterfall section.

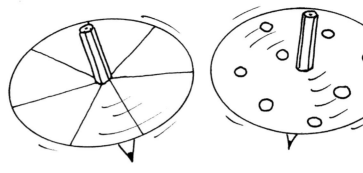

PSALM 65:9-13 COLLAGE

This passage describes how the rain which God sends waters the land and helps things to grow. Make a collage depicting a river, hills, trees, sheep, etc (see below). Use oval pieces of tissue paper for the river or stream, overlapping them as they are pasted on to the background. See p64 or **Templates** section for sheep outlines which can be covered in cotton wool or fabric remnants.

SKY PICTURES

This draws attention to the fascinating way in which the sky changes according to time of day and weather conditions. Using coloured paper or fabric and other materials help children make some of the following pictures, either as individuals or in small groups:

➜ **Sunny day:** blue sky; yellow sun; tiny, wispy, cotton wool clouds.
➜ **Night sky:** dark blue or black background; moon; silver stars.
➜ **Cloudy sky:** clouds cut from light grey paper; raindrops; umbrella (optional).
➜ **Starry sky:** dark grey background; large clouds; yellow/silver lightning flashes, rain.
➜ **Sunset sky:** pink, orange, yellow and pale blue background; large orange sun low in the sky; dark silhouette of house or tree in foreground.

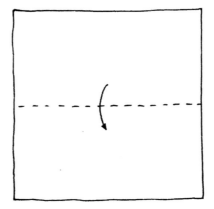

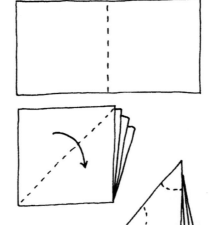

SNOWFLAKES

Uses: *for topics on weather, creation, variety and individuality – no two snowflakes, like no two people, are identical.*

This is an old favourite but one of which children never seem to tire, perhaps because the results are different each time. You can use squares or circles of white tissue or sugar paper or even kitchen paper (this, being absorbent, is best if you want to incorporate an activity involving colour).

Mount the snowflakes on a dark background for maximum effect.

1 Fold square of kitchen paper in half. Fold in half again.
2 Two sides of the square have only folds. Fold these together to make a triangle.
3 Cut out pieces from corners and edges.
4 Unfold to see your snowflake.

12 Sheep and shepherds

A SECTION devoted entirely to one species of animal and those who look after them may seem a little strange, but in fact sheep recur so often in Bible stories that many Bible topics include some reference to them.

Today, in a largely urban society, most of us see sheep only occasionally – perhaps when we are on holiday or make the effort to go out for a walk – but they were very much part of life in Bible times. Abraham, Lot and Jacob kept sheep, as did Moses after fleeing from Egypt. David, who started life as a shepherd boy and ended as the shepherd-king of Israel, gave us the most famous psalm of all which points to God as the supreme Shepherd. This image was brought to life – literally – by Jesus who, declaring himself 'the Good Shepherd', was also hailed by John the Baptist as 'the Lamb of God'.

We all have a sneaking affection for sheep, perhaps because we recognise the truth of the Bible's frequent comparisons of us, God's people, to them. Though figurative language of this kind is difficult for younger children to understand, older children can often appreciate that in many ways we are like sheep – sometimes stupid, wandering away and needing protection. So enjoy the 'sheepish' activities you find here!

SHEEPFOLD COLLAGE

You will need:
  Backing paper
  Glue
  Cotton wool and scraps of material
  Felt-tip pens
  Glue

This activity can be used with any sheep topic. Show a picture of an Eastern sheepfold, or describe one. Let children work individually or in groups to make a collage of the sheepfold, with sheep inside and a shepherd guarding the entrance.

SHEEPFOLD JUNK MODEL

Use boxes such as old cereal boxes to build the fold (if you cover them with plain paper first they are easier to stick together and paint). Make sheep from cardboard tubes covered with cotton wool and with white, brown, black or grey pipe-cleaner legs. Slot on pre-cut heads on which children have drawn eyes, nose and mouth. Each child can put his or her own sheep inside the sheepfold. A shepherd can be made (in advance if you wish) by standing a sturdy box on its end and covering it with fabric scraps. Glue on a circle of paper showing a face (add hair, a beard and moustache for extra effect), and add arms made from card and perhaps a crook, to either side of the box. Explain how the shepherd would sleep across the entrance to keep the sheep safe.

SLING, STAFF AND CROOK

You will need: a roll of lining paper; paints; crayons; materials for collaging.

Get a child to lie down on a large piece of lining paper and draw round him or her to get a silhouette. Ask the children to dress the figure as a shepherd, by painting, crayoning, or collaging. Fasten the figure to the wall at the group's eye height. Copy and enlarge the pictures of some of the equipment a shepherd would use to take care of sheep. Colour and cut them out and add to the picture.

SLEEPY SHEEP

You will need:

Large sheets of card (eg from grocery boxes)
Rolls of cotton wool
Slightly diluted PVA adhesive
Large brushes
Black paper eyes
Nose and mouth
The sheep outline as illustrated, to copy

Draw basic sheep outlines on the card and cut out, making the sheep as large as you can. Tease out the cotton wool so that it is quite thin. Give each child or group a pot of glue and brushes to spread it all over the card. Give a large piece of cotton wool to be laid across each pasted shape – don't trim any excess; press it on firmly to the body shape. Add features, then lean sheep against chairs, walls, etc to make them stand up.

SHEEP MASKS

1 Copy (and enlarge) the template onto thin card and cut out (cut out beforehand for very young children who can't manage scissors). Cover with cotton wool or colour in. Add paper strips for nose and mouth.
2 Fold between points A and B to give shaping.
3 Staple the face to a strip of card, measure and trim the band to fit the child.
4 Wear so that the sheep face rests above the child's forehead (some children don't like having their faces covered). Enjoy wearing the masks and making sheep noises.

For a simpler version:
Use large paper plates for masks. Cover with cotton wool, draw eyes and nose and cut out eyes. Tie masks on with wool.

SPECIAL SHEEP

This activity was designed originally to underline the fact that just as the Biblical shepherd knew his own sheep by name so we are known individually to the Good Shepherd. However it can also be used as a straightforward model-making activity.

Copy the illustration onto pieces of card and provide materials such as cotton wool for making the sheep's coat. Fold along dotted line to make your sheep stand up. (If using as a group activity, add a name collar to each sheep with the child's name on it.) Display in a long line by a wall, with a shepherd figure at the front.

See also:
- **Advent and Christmas** section for 'Shepherd Christmas cards' and 'Shepherd cardboard tube models'.
- **Angels** section for 'Glory all around'.
- **Recipes** section for 'Peppermint sheep' and 'Sheep cake or biscuits'.

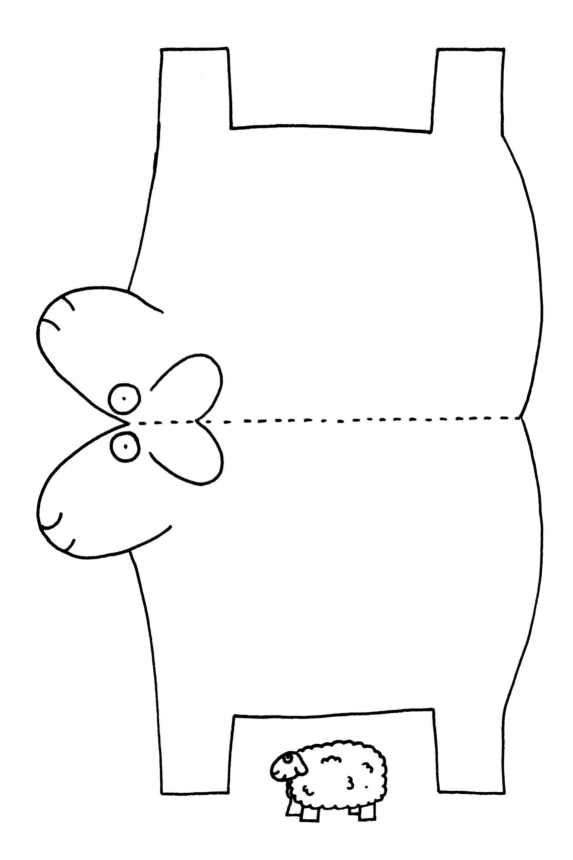

13 Birds

EAGLES and owls, doves and ravens, pigeons, partridges, quails, sparrows and swallows – just some of the birds which are mentioned in the Bible and which Jesus may well have had in mind when he told his listeners to consider the birds. Some of the most well-known and well-loved Bible stories feature birds — Noah, Elijah, the parable of the sower, the dove at Jesus' baptism.

Birds are mentioned in the Psalms as examples of God providing for his creatures, while the dove descending on Jesus at his baptism has given rise to the use of that bird as a symbol of the Holy Spirit. Birds are some of the most graceful and colourful of God's creatures and therefore very useful for craft activities such as posters and collages!

RAVEN FACES

(Use with story of ravens feeding Elijah or Noah sending out a raven from the ark.)

Follow instructions to make these faces. Younger children will need help with the actual construction but will enjoy experimenting with them once they are made.

1 Cut pieces opposite from stiff paper or thin card.
2 Fold top beak and paste to tabs on support as shown.
3 Fold bottom beak slightly along its length, then hook it over support and paste.
4 Paste or staple an eye on each side.

RAVEN

Uses:

Elijah and the ravens; Noah and the ark; Jesus' Sermon on the Mount; the parable of the sower.
Cut out template. Colour in beak and eyes on both sides. Stick small pieces of crepe paper (cut slightly fringed) for feathers and a small piece of white or yellow paper on to the beak to look like bread if you are using this for the story of Elijah being fed by ravens. Thread with string or cotton to hang.

TESSELLATING BIRD SHAPES

See illustration in **Pentecost** section.
NB For this to be an effective activity you will need plenty of the basic shape illustrated. Children could colour them before you work together to stick them up in an interesting display. (You could make a teaching point that God works to make us 'fit together' as Christians.)

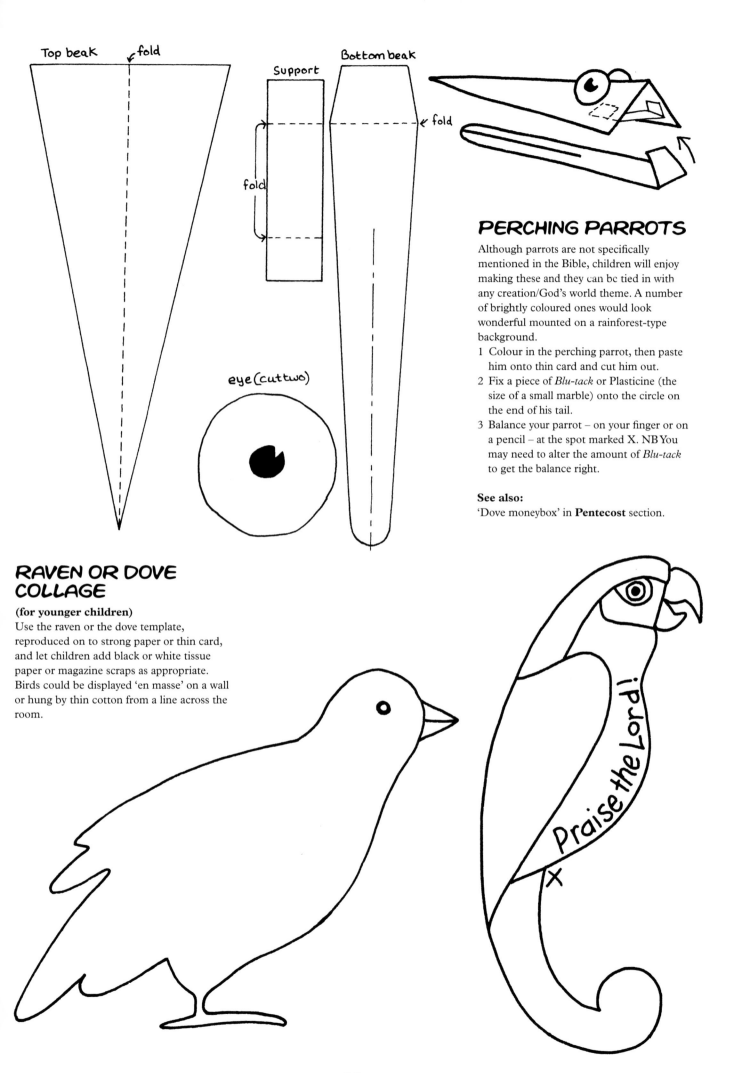

Top beak ← fold

Support

Bottom beak

fold

← fold

fold

eye (cut two)

PERCHING PARROTS

Although parrots are not specifically mentioned in the Bible, children will enjoy making these and they can be tied in with any creation/God's world theme. A number of brightly coloured ones would look wonderful mounted on a rainforest-type background.

1 Colour in the perching parrot, then paste him onto thin card and cut him out.

2 Fix a piece of *Blu-tack* or Plasticine (the size of a small marble) onto the circle on the end of his tail.

3 Balance your parrot – on your finger or on a pencil – at the spot marked X. NB You may need to alter the amount of *Blu-tack* to get the balance right.

See also:
'Dove moneybox' in **Pentecost** section.

RAVEN OR DOVE COLLAGE

(for younger children)
Use the raven or the dove template, reproduced on to strong paper or thin card, and let children add black or white tissue paper or magazine scraps as appropriate. Birds could be displayed 'en masse' on a wall or hung by thin cotton from a line across the room.

Praise the Lord!

X

14 Hands, feet and faces

CRAFT activities involving hands, feet and faces are always very popular, especially with younger children. Many of these activities are both colourful and 'tactile' (or just plain messy, depending on how positive we're feeling!). Because our hands, feet, faces and fingerprints are unique to us as individuals, activities to do with them, especially if the finished products are displayed or made distinctive in some way, can be very affirming —'You're special to God — there's no one else quite like you.' Hands and fingers also lend themselves to lots of puppet activities.

Craft activities on the subject of hands can be used in connection with stories of Jesus healing people, where the gospel writers frequently record that he touched them, with topics about helping, serving or caring for others, and with topics on the amazing nature of our bodies — how would we manage without thumbs, for example?

We are 'programmed' to recognise and respond to human faces at a very early stage in our lives. That fascination with people's faces and their varying expressions remains, and can be a rich source of activities and discussion: children love making faces and portraying different expressions and these can be used in talking about our own and other people's feelings.

Old hands (pardon the pun!) will recognise basic activities, some of which have been given a new twist, and you will also find here suggestions for tying in activities with particular Bible themes. Sections which may link with this section are **Hats and headgear** and **Bible people**.

HANDS POSTER

Draw round hands on coloured paper and cut out, or make handprints with paint, or cut out hands from magazines. Use in one of the following ways:

1 Paste on to a poster entitled 'Hands that help'.
2 Make a picture (see illustrations):
   Flower: Draw hands on yellow paper and cut out. Attach at wrist only, starting at edge and work towards centre. Attach an orange centre at the end.
   Hedgehog: Cut hands from brown paper. Attach at back first and work towards head. Attach the head last.
   Tree: Cut hands from green paper (different shades of green can be quite effective). Attach at the bottom first and work up.
3 Sketch two giant praying hands on the background and fill with cut out hand shapes.

HOLDING HANDS FRIEZE

Tape hand shapes together, with alternate fingers and wrists touching and display with an appropriate verse or caption (see illustration). This, like the other hand ideas above, could be made into a banner by using material rather than paper and mounting handshapes on to a piece of background material.

HANDS PLAQUE

Give each child a rolled-out square of bought or homemade baking clay (see recipe on page 4) or let them roll it out. Make a flat handprint in the square. Push a ring opener from a soft drinks can into the top for a hanger and let the child write his/her name in the clay using a matchstick. Bake till hardened.

HANDPRINTS

Handprints can be made using clay (see recipe on page 4) or in paint. Fingerprints can also be used to make pictures, especially of creatures like tadpoles, caterpillars and birds. (See **God's world** section.)

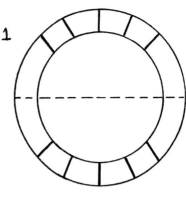

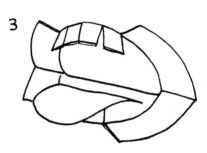

MAKE A MOUTH

You will need:

    Paper plates or circles of card
    Half circles of red paper
    Glue or sticky tape

1 Fold plates in half and cut along thick black lines to make slits for teeth.
2 Fold teeth down from top and up from bottom.
3 Stick red semicircle inside mouth for tongue, then make it 'talk' or 'sing'.

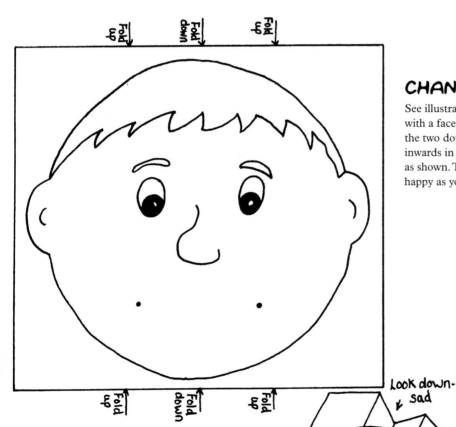

CHANGE A FACE

See illustration. Photocopy and cut out the square with a face in it. Draw a straight mouth between the two dots and colour in the face. Fold the paper inwards in half first, and then the two sides outwards as shown. The face is sad as you look down and happy as you look up.

FOOTPRINTS

Generally speaking, footprints can be made in a similar way to handprints, except that it is slightly more complicated and messy to do painted footprints. You will need to be more organised and have plenty of helpers and bowls of warm water (big enough to wash feet in) ready afterwards.

Feet and footprint craft activities can be used in connection with:

→ stories about journeys – since walking was the most common means of travel in Bible times.

→ stories about lameness (eg Mephibosheth; the lame man at the Beautiful Gate; the man at the pool of Bethesda).

→ topics about the wonders of our bodies and the joy of being able to use our feet and legs.

MAKING FACES 1

Children enjoy making faces with different expressions and these can be made in a variety of ways:

➜ Model from play dough or plasticine, using buttons, dried pasta, drinking straws and string to make features.
➜ Provide paper plates, felt-tip pens and wool or wood-shavings (for hair) to tape on. If the plates are not shiny you could create a different expression front and back. (Paper plate faces also lend themselves to becoming stick puppets by attaching a piece of dowelling to the back.)
➜ Paint faces in strong colours on paper bags – these can work as 'glove' puppets.

MAKE FACES 2

Use one and a half paper plates for each face.

1 Draw a happy face on the plate.
2 Draw a sad mouth on the spare half.
3 Use sticky tape to fix the two halves together (see illustration). Flip up to draw eyes to go with the happy mouth.

1.

2.

3.

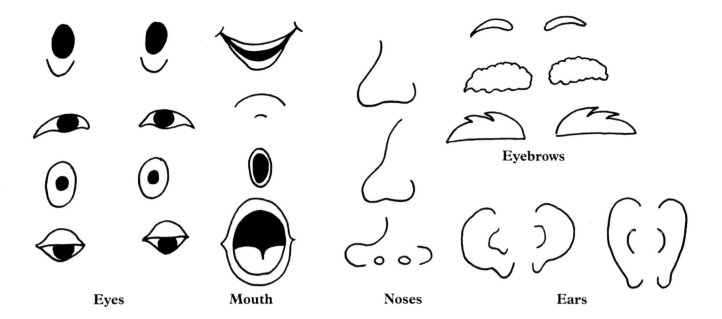

Eyes   **Mouth**   **Noses**   **Ears**

Eyebrows

SHOW YOUR FEELINGS!

You will need:
  Face-shaped pieces of paper
  Enlarged copies of the facial features
    (above)
  Glue sticks
  Scissors

Experiment with making different expressions. Faces could be used to make a mobile.

SPECTACULAR SPECS

Photocopy this pattern onto thick paper or thin card and cut out. (You may need to have done this beforehand if you have younger children. A craft knife is the best way to cut out the eyeholes, so it's safest if an adult does that anyway.) Put a lump of plasticine underneath the card and use a compass or pencil point to make small holes at the side and thread shirring elastic through.

Decorate the specs adventurously. Use as an activity for any 'seeing' theme, and change the verse accordingly.

15 Hats and headgear

I RECENTLY gave a talk at an infant school and at lunchtime the staff excitedly showed me their costumes for 'Book Week' when both children and staff dress up as fictional characters. The Reception class teacher tried on her Alice in Wonderland outfit, a classroom assistant became Red Riding Hood's grandma with a grey wig and mob cap, and the school's only male teacher tossed his long 'Captain Hook' locks, scowling fiercely as Bo-Peep, Robin Hood and Jack and Jill waited to look in the mirror. I realised again we all love dressing up!

Children love it even more than adults! A huge part of their learning comes through imitating and copying older people, and there is certainly a role-play element in dressing-up games. There is also the novelty of wearing garments different from normal attire and learning to negotiate things like high heels and long skirts. Even more importantly, as children dress up they learn what it is like to 'be' someone else – vital if they are to be able to see someone else's point of view.

Sadly, most of our Sunday groups don't have time for full-scale dressing-up, but very often a hat will do. Hats have enormous significance in our culture – think of the number of expressions where we use the word hat: 'if the cap fits, wear it'; 'old hat' and the expression, 'wears several different hats', meaning 'has several different roles'. Headgear can be a good alternative to dressing up 'properly'.

You will find in this section several very simple hats which can be made from newspaper, sugar paper or even wallpaper, and which will all be much appreciated by wearers and spectators alike. Some link with **Bible people**, some with **Praise and celebration** and there are sheep masks in the **Sheep and shepherds** section.

CROWNS

Uses: *for stories about kings, queens, princes, or to focus on King Jesus, or on the fact that as Christians we are 'kings and priests'.*
The simplest crowns can be made two at a time – see illustration. Decorate with felt-tips, with sequins, glitter, etc. or by writing on an appropriate verse. Secure the hat with paperclips or staples (remembering to put some sticky tape over the sharp ends of the staples).

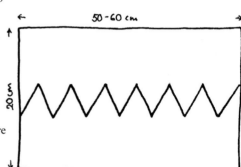

EAR, EAR!

Use a strip of card to make a headband. Photocopy the ear templates and cut them out. Cut along the line shown. Overlap the edges so that one x is over the other and staple. Attach ears to headband. (This can also be used in conjunction with `faces').

This basic method – ears on a cardboard headband – is a good way of suggesting all sorts of different animals – from rabbits to elephants.

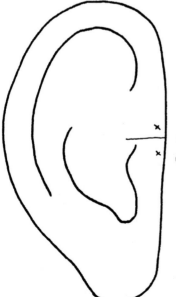

PRIEST'S HAT

1 Fold in half a sheet of (news)paper approximately 60cm/22 inches square.
2 Turn up one side about 5cm.
3 Turn over and fold sides to centre.
4 Fold bottom flap upwards.
5 Staple or paste flap in place.

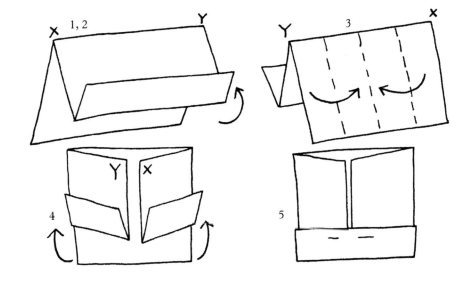

PARTY HATS

Make party hats using stiff card or wallpaper (avoid ready-pasted wallpaper which has fungicide in the paste), and decorate as desired with crepe paper rosettes (see page 88), streamers, glitter, etc.

Straight hats :

1 Fold a large piece of paper in half. Cut off the corners.
2 Staple the sides of the hat as shown and fold up the bottom edges of the hat.

Round hats :

1 Cut a large circle 38cm/15 inches in diameter.
2 Shape hat to head size, and staple in place.

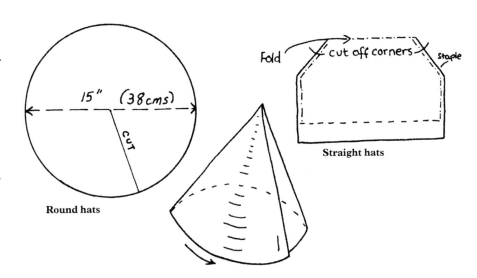

15" (38cms)

CUT

Round hats

Fold   cut off corners   staple

Straight hats

OFFICIAL HATS

This is a quick and simple way of suggesting 'official' hats for young children or perhaps for a mime or sketch. The method given can be adapted for a policeman, nurse, soldier, chef – in fact anyone who can be identified by their headgear.

For each hat you will need:
A strip of card (to fit each child's head)
A template shape (see diagram)
Scissors
Glue
A stapler

Fireman's hat

1 Cut out the shape.
2 Fix to the band and decorate or colour.
3 Fit to the child's head.

TWO PAPER HATS

Simple hat

1 Fold a large rectangle of paper in half.
2 Fold the two top corners as shown. This will leave two flaps at the bottom.
3 Fold one of the bottom flaps upwards, over the corners.
4 Turn the hat over to the other side and do the same again.

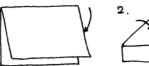

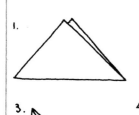 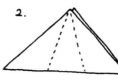 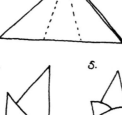

Fancy hat

(will need some adult help)

1 Fold a large square of paper in half diagonally.
2 Divide the bottom edge of the triangle into three. Mark the sections with a pencil and draw lines from the top point of the triangle to your marks. Fold the left side of the triangle in so that its edge lies along the pencil line on the right.
3 Fold the right side of the triangle over the left side.
4 Fold the two pointed sections at the bottom of the hat upwards on the same side. Keep them in place with sticky tape.
5 Pull the hat open and wear it!

PAPER PLATE HALOES

This is a quick and easy way to suggest angels if you want to get away from tinsel! Children can decorate these before wearing them if they wish.

Make a card headband as described above, and staple to it, at the back, a paper plate (plain or decorated) so that the upper side of the plate faces forward and shows above the children's head.

EASTERN SHEPHERDS' HEADDRESSES

We all know that the best way to make these is to raid the tea towel drawer! However, keeping them in place can be a bit tricky. The best solution is to use the waistband cut from a discarded pair of ladies' tights! These are just the right width for the tea towel to be tucked into at the front, and are stretchy and comfortable as well.

COINS HEADDRESS

Uses: *in connection with weddings or parties or Luke's story of the lost coin or any topic where the teaching point is that we are of value in God's eyes.*

Follow the instructions on the diagram to make either version of this.

Simple coin headdress

1 Cut a piece of card long enough to go round a child's head. Cover with foil.
2 Tape the card into a band to fit child.
3 Tie on 10 foil circles (milk bottle tops). Add more sparkle with glitter or glitter glue.

Fancy coin headdress

Photocopy the coins shown. Colour with yellow or metallic crayons. Pick out the letters with glitter or glitter glue. Make a band as above. Mount the coins on thick cardboard and hang in letter order to spell out 'Jesus loves'.

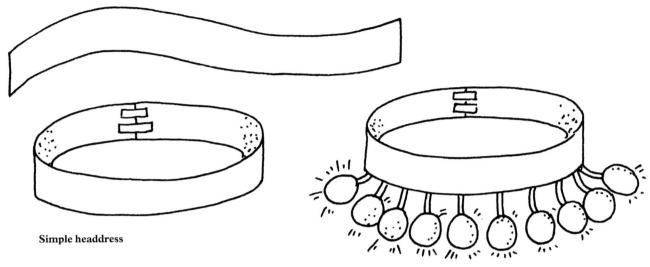

Simple headdress

Fancy headdress

75

16 Recipes

FOOD, glorious food! Cooking must rank high on the 'favourite activities' list of many children. It may be because generally speaking they have such healthy appetites (which is a polite way of saying they're always 'starving') but I think it's also because cooking is a wonderful example of Paul's words that 'God gives us richly all things to enjoy'. It's such a satisfying activity because it involves so many of our senses: touch, sight, smell, taste and even hearing (the sound of something sizzling in a pan is sometimes enough to set the mouth watering, isn't it?). Most of the recipes below could be used in connection with the **Praise and celebration** section. So roll up your sleeves and get busy!

A FEW TIPS

Time and energy-savers

Instead of laboriously and messily greasing baking trays, invest in a couple of rolls of black non-stick lining paper (available in supermarkets, usually with the cling film and cooking foil). It's about £4 for a 1 metre roll, but you can re-use it dozens of times, and cut it to fit trays and tins. Everything cooks well on it – even pizzas dripping with cheese lift off easily, after which you can wash or rinse the sheet and use it again. It's brilliant.

Breadmaking

→ Some recipes suggest live yeast, which isn't always easy to come by. The best substitute is 'easy-blend' yeast, which you just mix into the dry ingredients. If you are used to the old type of dried yeast, which had to be mixed with sugar and water, read the instructions carefully!

→ Adding water to flour: all flours differ in how much water they absorb, so the amounts of water given in bread recipes are always approximate; you need to add water very gradually and you should end up with a smooth dough which leaves the sides of the bowl clean.

Melting chocolate

This is best done in an ovenproof bowl over a pan of hot water. The problems start if you overheat it or get water into it, when it turns into something resembling chocolate flake, and cannot be reversed! You can also melt chocolate in a microwave but you need the lowest setting (Defrost or equivalent) and make sure you do it in short bursts – about 30 seconds at a time.

Biscuits

After taking biscuits out of the oven, you should always leave them to cool for a few minutes before moving them to a wire cooling rack. If you try to lift them immediately they will be too soft and will break up.

SAFETY CONSIDERATIONS

There are a few basic safety rules when cooking with young children:

→ Make sure you know beforehand if any child in the group has a food allergy or sensitivity, eg to food colouring, or if there are any foods which they are not permitted to eat, such as meat or sweets. (It's useful to get this information as soon as a child joins the group and to record it where it's easily accessible, eg in a card index.) Be careful with products containing nuts or colouring and don't let children lick out bowls which have had raw eggs in them. (You may prefer to use dried egg white for recipes not needing whole eggs.)

→ Cook in *small* groups. Generally speaking, the younger the children, the more adult help you need, and the smaller the group needs to be. Two or three under-fives cooking at once is more than enough!

→ Make sure hands are washed and clothes protected before you start.

→ Don't expect children to cook at worktop heights designed for adults – if possible use low tables, covered with plastic cloths.

→ For convenience organise and prepare ingredients in advance. Children enjoy mixing, decorating and tasting, so concentrate on those bits of the process.

→ Try to start with as much room and as little clutter as possible.

→ Don't let children use sharp knives, skewers or tin openers, and watch young children with cocktail sticks.

→ Remind children, before you begin, of the need to follow instructions exactly and not to run or rush about when cooking.

PARTY FOOD

Mini-pizzas

(for those with access to a grill or microwave)

Cut a French stick into thin slices. Supply a variety of toppings, eg cheese, chopped ham, small pieces of cooked sausage. Spread each slice with a little tomato sauce, passata or puree and let children create their own toppings. Cook under a medium grill for a few minutes (or in a microwave oven for about 30 seconds) until the cheese is melted and meat heated through. If more time is available, baking the pizzas in an oven would give a crispier base. *Conversation topics while cooking could include: Jesus gave bread to hungry people; God provides us with food.*

Apple boats

You will need:
- Firm eating apples
- Wooden cocktail sticks
- Paper triangles
- Lime jelly (made beforehand)

Method: Cut an apple into quarters and remove the core. Make sails from cocktail sticks and paper triangles (if small children are involved, cut off one sharp end and stick the other point into the apple.) Chop up the lime jelly to make a sea for the apple boats.

Party mallows

(no cooking required)
You will need:
- Marshmallows
- Pre-melted chocolate
- Sugar strands (in bowls)
- Forks

Method: Spear marshmallows onto forks, and dip first into melted chocolate then into sugar strands.

Red Fruit Punch

You will need:
- Cranberry juice
- Red grape juice
- Apple juice
- Sweet black grapes
- Large bowl
- Sparkling water or lemonade (optional)

Method: Cut grapes in half and remove pips. Mix equal amounts of the fruit juices together. Add sparkling drink if desired. Pour out and add a few pieces of grape to each cup.

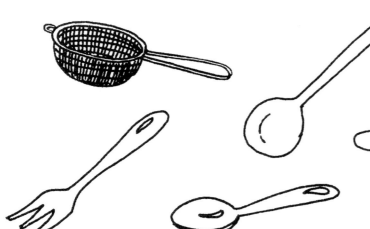

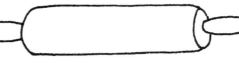

Marzipan fruits

(no cooking required)
NB As marzipan is made from almonds, check for nut allergies.

You will need:
- Marzipan (preferably white)
- Food colouring
- Cloves (optional)
- Icing sugar or fine cornflour
- Flat plates if you have no suitable working surface
- Petits fours cases

Method: Colour pieces of marzipan with food colouring – this can be done beforehand if you are short of time. Give each child a piece of marzipan and show them how to mould into small fruits such as oranges, apples, plums, cherries and bananas. Inserting a clove into one end of fruits like apples or oranges makes them look very authentic, and rolling the 'fruit' against

the part of a grater used for nutmegs gives the mottled appearance of orange skin. Finished fruits can be placed in petits fours cases. Store in an airtight container.

Fruity flapjacks

You will need:
- 120g margarine
- 50g demerara sugar
- 50ml golden syrup
- 250g porridge oats
- 175g dried fruit
- Shallow greased baking tray

Method: Preheat oven to Gas Mark 4/ 180°C/ 350°F. Melt the margarine, sugar and syrup together in a small saucepan or microwave. Stir the oats and fruit together in a large bowl, carefully pour on the sugar mixture and stir well. Tip mixture into the greased tin. Press down and smooth the surface. Cook for 15 minutes. Leave to cool and then mark on cutting lines. When the flapjack is cool and firm, break along these lines.

Tiffin

You will need:
- 4oz/100g margarine
- 4oz/100g sugar
- 1 beaten egg
- 1 tbsp cocoa powder
- 8oz/200g crushed digestive biscuits
- 6oz /150g bar of chocolate (approximately 3 regular-sized bars)
- Greased traybake/Swiss roll tin

Method: Melt margarine in a pan over a low heat. Add sugar and stir until dissolved. Remove from heat, add beaten egg and stir well. Add cocoa powder and crushed biscuits. Spread in tin to thickness required. Cook at Gas Mark 3-4 for 10-15 minutes. Leave to cool, and when still warm, cover with melted chocolate or chocolate glace icing and leave to set.

CHRISTMAS

Candle cakes

You will need:
- Ready made small sponge cakes
- Glacé icing
- Sweets
- Chocolate strands, etc for decorating

Method: Cover small cakes with glace icing and decorate with jelly sweets, chocolate strands, etc. Put a birthday candleholder and small candle in the centre of each as a reminder that Christmas is a time to celebrate the birthday of Jesus.

Star biscuits

You will need:
- Biscuit dough (see page 80)
- Flour
- Rolling pins and star cutters

Method: Either make the bisuits from scratch (if you have an oven) or decorate ready-baked star-shaped biscuits with thick glace icing, cherries, hundreds and thousands, silver balls, etc.

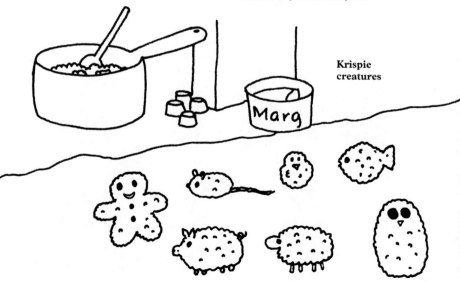

Krispie creatures

Marg

CRISPY RECIPES

Krispie creatures

You will need:
- 2-3 cups of Rice Krispies
- 50g margarine
- 250g marshmallows
- Currants and dried fruit for making features

Method: Melt the margarine in a saucepan or microwave. Add the marshmallows and stir until melted. Add enough Rice Krispies to make a stiff consistency. Turn mixture out in small quantities on to pieces of lightly greased foil. Whilst it is still warm but not hot, let children mould it into animals or people, using currants etc. for eyes and so on.

Crispy cakes

(no cooking required – makes about 12)
You will need:
- 110g cooking chocolate (or use golden syrup and cocoa)
- 150g cornflakes
- Bowl of hot water
- Extra bowl
- Paper cake cases
- Spoon

Method: Melt the chocolate in a bowl placed over the bowl of hot water or in a microwave. Let children stir in cornflakes until they are all well-covered (cornflakes not children, that is!). Spoon the mixture into cake cases and leave to cool.

Sticky krispies

You will need:
- 100g toffee
- 100g margarine
- 100g marshmallows
- 100g Rice Krispies

Method: Melt together the toffee, margarine and marshmallows (most easily done in a microwave) and stir in Rice Krispies. Press into a greased baking tray and leave to cool. Cut into pieces to eat.

JEWISH/PASSOVER RECIPES AND BREAD

Pretend Plavah

You will need:
Cooked pastry base (or sponge flan, but that might not be unleavened!)
- 150ml whipping cream★
- 150ml Greek yoghurt★
- Tin of strawberries (or fresh strawberries if you prefer)
- Strawberry jam
- 2 or 3 meringue nests

Method: Whip the cream until thick. Fold in the yoghurt and drained strawberries. Spread the jam over the pastry base centre. Turn the mixture into the flan case. Crush the meringue nests and sprinkle on the top.

- For a simpler (and cheaper!) version try using a packet whip, such as strawberry, instead of the yoghurt and cream.

Jewish bread

(makes approx 12 rolls)
You will need:
- 50g margarine
- 500g strong plain flour
- 20g caster sugar
- 1 medium egg
- 1 sachet of easy-blend yeast
- 185ml tepid water
- 5g salt
- Sesame/poppy seeds
- Greased baking sheet

Method: Preheat oven to Gas Mark 8/ 230°C/450°F. Sieve flour into basin, rub in margarine. Add dried yeast and mix in well. Mix sugar, salt and egg together. Add all other ingredients, including water, to the flour mixture and mix to form a rough dough. Turn out on to a floured working surface and knead and flatten for about 10 minutes. Divide the dough into strands and twist together. Place on a greased baking sheet and cover with a cloth. Leave in a warm place for 45 minutes, until the dough doubles in size. Brush the tops with milk; decorate with seeds and bake for 20-25 minutes.

Unleavened bread

You will need:

- 225g plain flour
- 50g hard margarine cut into small pieces
- 150ml hot water
- Rolling pin
- Frying pan

Method: Rub the fat into the flour by hand. Add hot water until dough is pliable but not sticky. Divide into ten balls and roll each one out until it's about 10 cm across. Cook in a frying pan, without oil, for at least 30 seconds each side.

Sweet bread

You will need:

- 500g/1lb of strong plain flour (the kind sold for breadmaking)
- 50g/2oz sugar
- 1 sachet easy-blend dried yeast
- 50g/2oz butter or margarine, cut into small pieces
- 120ml/4 fluid oz warm milk (blood heat)
- 120ml/4 fluid oz warm water

Method: Rub the fat into the flour. Add remaining dry ingredients and mix well. Add the liquids, stir in and knead well. If you have time at this stage, allow dough to rise (covered) in a warm place until it has doubled in size, before re-kneading briefly and shaping into rolls – you will get a smoother, lighter textured dough.

Shape as required, in knots, twists, crescents, etc before baking at 220°C/450°F for 10-15 minutes. These sweet dough rolls can be iced with water icing and decorated with chocolate or sugar strands.

BISCUITS

Basic biscuit recipe

You will need:

- 200g/8oz self-raising flour
- 100g/4oz margarine
- 100g/4oz sugar
- 1 egg
- Vanilla essence
- Greased baking tray

Method:

Stage 1: Preheat oven to Gas Mark 4/ 180°C/350°F. Cream the margarine and sugar until soft.

Stage 2: Add the egg and a few drops of vanilla essence.

Stage 3: Sift the flour and add to the mixture, making a stiff dough then roll mixture into balls and flatten slightly. Bake for 10-15 minutes.

Variations

- **Honey biscuits**
Add 15g honey at end of stage 2.
- **Manna biscuits**
Add 50g honey at end of stage 2.
- **Fog's biscuits**
Add 75g desiccated coconut at end of stage 3.
- **Egg biscuits** (for Easter)
At end of stage 3 split the mixture in two. Work a little food colouring roughly into each half to give a marbled effect. Cut out with an oval cutter, after either rolling the two halves back together or rolling them separately.

Melting moments

You will need:

- 100g margarine
- 75g sugar
- 150g self-raising flour
- A few drops of vanilla essence
- Half an egg or 1 egg yolk
- Crushed cornflakes or rolled oats
- A few cherries
- Greased baking trays

Method: Cream together the margarine and sugar. Add the vanilla essence and egg, then the sieved flour. Knead the mixture into a firm, smooth dough and divide it into small balls. Roll the balls in crushed cornflakes and place, slightly flattened, on greased baking trays. Space them out fairly well to allow for spreading. Decorate each biscuit with a piece of cherry.

Bake at Gas Mark 5/190°C/375°F, for 15-20 minutes. Leave to cool on trays for a few minutes and then lift the biscuits onto a wire cooling rack, using a pallet knife or fish slice.

Chocolate chip cookies

You will need:

- 100g margarine
- 100g sugar
- 200g flour
- 1 tbsp milk
- 1 tbsp golden syrup
- 1 tsp bicarbonate of soda
- 50g chocolate drops or chopped chocolate
- Greased baking trays

Method: Cream together the margarine and sugar. Heat milk and syrup together gently, then add, alternately with sieved flour and bicarbonate of soda, to the creamed mixture. Fold in the chocolate chips. Roll the mixture into small balls and place on greased baking trays. Press the balls flat with a fork. Bake at Gas Mark 2/150°C/330°F for 25 minutes or until golden brown.

Stained glass windows

These are very simple, but look spectacular.
You will need:
200g/8oz self-raising flour
100g/4oz castor sugar
100g/4oz margarine
1 beaten egg
A squeeze of lemon juice
150g/6oz crushed boiled sweets (place in polythene bag, cover with tea towel and bash with rolling pin)
Baking tray
Oiled greaseproof paper (optional)
Rolling pin

Method: Mix together the flour and sugar. Rub in the margarine. Mix to stiff dough with the egg and lemon juice. Knead well and then roll the dough out. Cut it into 15-20 window shapes using the template or a round cutter (don't forget to cut a hole in the centre). Place the shapes on a baking tray or oiled greaseproof paper to prevent sticking. Fill the centres with crushed sweets. Bake for about 15 minutes at Gas Mark 4. Allow to cool completely before peeling the paper off.

Variation

Crown biscuits

Cut out biscuits (see above recipe) using a crown-shaped cutter, and make small holes in the biscuits. Fill with crushed sweets, and cook. When they have been baked the crowns will have 'jewels' in them!

St Nicholas biscuits

(makes 20-40 biscuits)
You will need:
120g caster sugar
50g margarine
180g plain flour
5g baking powder (1 level teaspoon)
1 egg, well–beaten
A few drops of vanilla essence
A few drops of milk
Greased baking tray

Method: Cream the sugar and margarine together. Add other dry ingredients. Mix with egg, vanilla essence and milk to form stiff dough, adding more flour if necessary.

Cut into letter* or Christmas shapes and put onto a lightly greased baking tray. Bake in a hot oven for 10-15 minutes.

*It was traditional in Holland to give people letter-shaped biscuits to celebrate the arrival of St Nicholas in the first week of December – hence the name of this recipe.

Peppermint sheep

Leader's preparations: Make the peppermint mixture beforehand by mixing 12 heaped tablespoons of sieved icing sugar into an egg white which has been whisked until frothy. Add a few drops of peppermint essence and knead on a surface dusted with icing sugar. Cut shapes A and B (see illustration) one for each child. Give each child a piece of greaseproof paper, lightly dusted with icing sugar.

Put shape A on to the paper, moisten the shaded area and add shape B, overlapping where moistened. Mark ear and mouth with a skewer. Add a sultana or currant for eye. Complete by adding chocolate sticks (such as Matchmakers) for legs. Leave to dry.

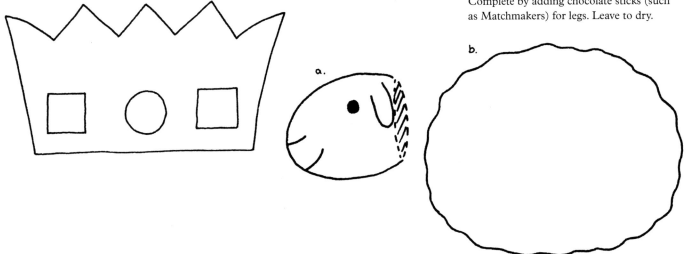

Sheep cake or biscuits

Leader's preparations: Provide plain biscuits or flat slices of plain cake for each child. Make up some green icing. Give the children blunt knives and let them cover the biscuits or cake with the icing.

Place a peppermint sheep (see above) made earlier by adults, on each biscuit or cake. Let the children add legs and eyes as shown.

17 Bits and bobs

This section is really a hotchpotch of activities that I didn't want to leave out, but which didn't fit neatly into any of the other categories – have fun!

PAPER LANTERNS

Uses: *any topic on 'light' or 'celebration'.*
These lanterns are simple to make but can be very effective, as endless variations are possible depending on the size and type of paper you use. String them up to give a room an instant festive look.

1 Fold a rectangular sheet of paper in half.
2 Cut from the fold towards the edge of the paper but stop about 1 inch from the edge.
3 Open out the sheet of paper, curl it round and tape the two ends together.

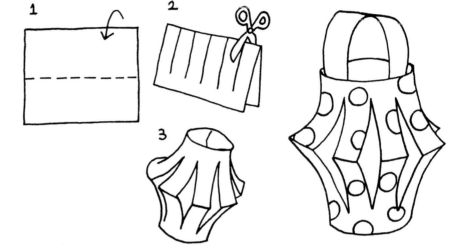

MARBLED BOOKMARKS

Marbling fascinates children and gives impressive results. These bookmarks could be given as gifts, eg for Mothering Sunday. You can also use the marbling method to make cards instead of bookmarks, or use a different verse to use the activity with a different theme.

You will need:
  Strips of paper 6cm wide
  Scissors; a bowl of water
  Two or three colours of oil-based paint or ink
  A stirrer
  Coloured crayons
  Pens or paint
  A glue stick
(There are also marbling kits available from craft and toy shops.)

Try this out fully before doing it with children. If time is limited, do stage 1 beforehand.

1 Cut two strips of paper, the same size. Cut out the middle of one strip of paper to make the frame: 1 cm wide at the side edges, 2cm deep at the ends.
2 Put 2-3cm depth of water in the bowl.
3 Add drops of two or three colours of oil-based paints or inks. Swirl gently.
4 Put the frame on the surface for a second and carefully lift off again.
5 Leave it to dry.
6 Use a second strip of paper to draw on your bookmark design, avoiding the edges.
7 When dry, stick the frame on top.

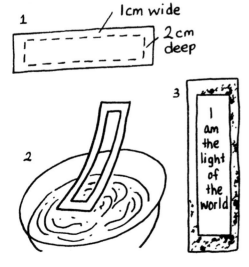

MEXICAN STAR

This activity was originally designed to help children remember to pray for Mexico; it could also be adapted, using sparkly materials or narrow shiny gift ribbon, as a Christmas activity.

You will need:
  Two drinking straws or kebab sticks for each child
  Sticky tape
  Small balls of coloured yarn
  Demonstrate how to make a diamond pattern by passing the yarn over one of the arms of the cross, then round it, before going over the next arm, rotating the cross as you work. Change colours to make stripes. Fasten ends of yarn with sticky tape and tie on new yarn. Cover the knot and tape, as you wind the yarn round. Fix loops with sticky tape and hang the stars up to display.

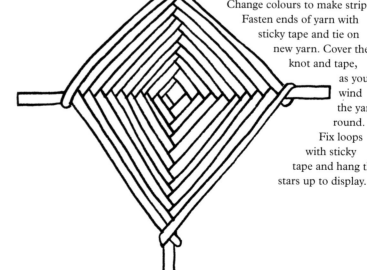

Leave at least 1cm at each end

C | All things were created by God's Son and | D
corner A ← 30 cm or longer → corner B

A _____ B

A | everything was made for him. Colossians 1:16 | B

MÖBIUS MEMORY VERSE

(suitable only for older children)
Uses: *for topics on eternity or eternal life or simply to help learn any memory verse.*
1 Write half the memory verse on one side of the paper, leaving at least 1 cm at each end. Words can be decorated.
2 The way you turn the paper over is very important! Keeping the long edge at the bottom where it is, turn the paper towards you. The writing will be upside down on the underside.
3 Write the second part of the memory verse on this side.
4 Make one twist in the paper and bring the ends together. Glue them in place.
5 Starting at the beginning, read your memory verse without stopping!

POM-POM PALS

This is another old favourite which even small children can make with some adult help. Young children will complete a pom-pom quicker if the centre hole is not too big and if they are given fairly thick wool to use. Once the pom-poms are made, they can be decorated and made into 'creatures' to give as gifts.

Wool can be one colour or several different colours – join with a knot.
1 Cut two circles of stiff card. Cut out the centres.
2 Hold two pieces together and start to wind wool round the card, going through the hole.
3 Let the child continue to wind the wool until it is 5 or 6 layers thick or the hole is full.
4 An adult cuts wool all around, keeping the lower blade between pieces of card.
5 Tie a length of wool tightly round the cut lengths, going between the card pieces.
6 Peel off the cards.
7 Fluff out the pom-pom and stick on the label and features with PVA glue.

84

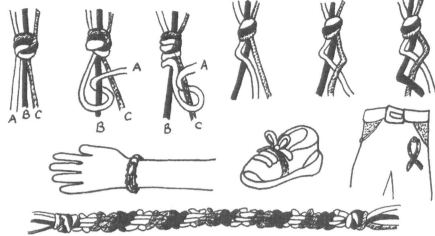

write a verse on the silhouette, using their own name, eg 'Don't be afraid Susi, I have called you by name...' Paste the silhouettes to the wallpaper to make a frieze. Spray the hairspray lightly on to the writing to stop the chalk from smudging.

MAKE A DIVER

Uses: *with older children as an extra activity with any water topic.*

You will need:

A plastic pen top (with safety hole)
Blu-tack
Large clear plastic bottle with lid

1 Make a diver by plugging the safety hole at the top of a plastic pen top with *Blu-tack* or plasticine. Add sufficient to make diver float upright.

2 Fill a long clear plastic bottle with water nearly to the top. Float diver inside and screw top on tightly. Squeeze bottle and watch diver dive. Release and let him surface.

FRIENDSHIP STRINGS

Uses: *themes on friendship or on The Trinity (if you use 3 strands).*

These are very popular with both boys and girls. They can be worn as bracelets, necklaces, shoelaces or just as ornaments. As the directions suggest, you could include a red thread as a reminder of Jesus' love in dying for us and you could also encourage the more skilful or experienced members of the group to help the novices. The strings can be made as gifts.

Use three strands of embroidery thread or wool about 70cm long.

1 Tie the threads together, about 5cm from one end. Pin or tape the loose ends down.

2 Hold thread B with your left hand. Loop thread A over the top, and then underneath, as shown. Pull the loop you have made up to the knot at the top. Do exactly the same again, looping thread A over and under thread B.

3 Now do the same thing, this time taking thread A over thread C. Again, do it twice. Thread B should be at the left hand side now.

4 Carry on in the same way, always knotting the left hand thread twice round the centre thread, then twice round the right hand thread. Stop when your string is long enough. Tie all the threads together and trim the ends about 5cm from the knot.

Simpler strings can be made by plaiting, like this:

- Take the left hand thread over the middle thread.
- Then take the right hand thread over the middle thread.
- Carry on taking the left hand and right hand threads alternately.

You can tie strings to make bracelets, or wear them in any way you want. You can give them to a friend.

SILHOUETTES

You will need:

A bright lamp (an angle-poise lamp is ideal)
Large sheets of black paper
Roll of wallpaper
Chalk
Scissors
Glue
Hairspray
Blu-tack
Copies of any verse about God's concern for us as individuals
Extra people to help

If your group is large, give those waiting to be silhouetted another activity to occupy them as they wait. Each child in turn stands close to the paper, as shown, with the shadow of his or her head falling onto it. With chalk, draw round the outline of their silhouette. Then give the child the paper on which you have drawn so that they can cut round the silhouette. Using chalk they can then

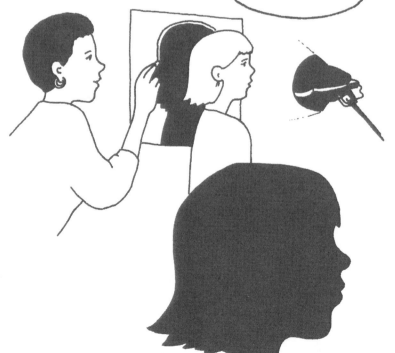

M-PHONES!

(megaphone, microphone, mobile phone)
Uses: *for topics on 'communication' of all kinds.*

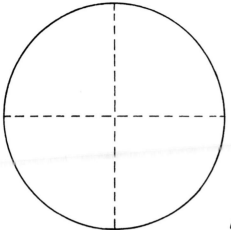

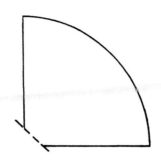

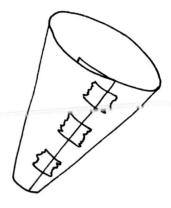

Make a megaphone

You will need:
  Sugar paper
  Scissors
  Sticky tape

1 Cut a large circle into quarters.
2 Snip off 'point' of quarter.
3 Roll up quarter and secure with tape.

Make a microphone

You will need:
  Cardboard roll
  Ball of newspaper
  Square of thin foam packing
  Piece of string
  Sticky tape
  PVA glue.
1 Wrap the paper in the foam and tape round 'stalk'.
2 Push the foam into tube. A line of PVA glue on the inside of the tube will secure the foam.
3 Tape a piece of string to the base.

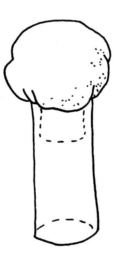

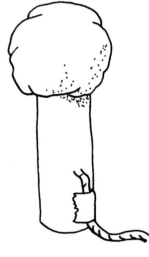

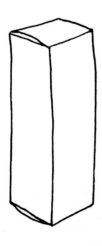

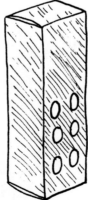

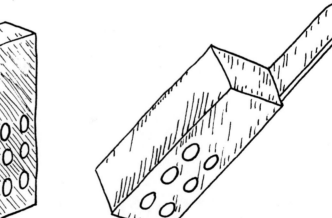

Make a mobile phone

You will need:
  Empty toothpaste box
  Black paint
  Sticky tap
  Self adhesive spots
  Lolly stick

1 Seal ends of box and paint box and lolly stick black.
2 When dry, stick on spots and add lolly stick as aerial.

CRAFTY COLOURS

4 ideas

NB Make sure you protect the table, the floor and your clothes from splashes.

Colour spots

You will need:

> Absorbent paper, eg blotting paper or good kitchen roll
> Poster paint (not too thick)
> A paint brush for each colour

1 Dip the brush into the paint. Touch the centre of the paper and watch the colour spread.
2 Dry the paper a little, eg with a hairdryer.
3 Dip a brush into a second colour. Again touch the centre of the page.
4 Partially dry again and repeat with a third colour.

Paint blowing

You will need:

> Non-absorbent paper
> Poster paint (not too thick)
> A drinking straw, a paint brush.

1 Use the brush to put a drop of paint on the surface of the paper.
2 Blow it along the paper gently with the drinking straw.
3 Add more colours, starting from the same or different places.

Chromatography

You will need:

> Filter paper or good blotting paper
> A variety of pens or inks
> A dropper
> Water
> A beaker

1 Make a small spot in the centre of the paper, with a pen or ink.
2 Dry it by waving the paper around.

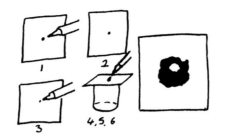

Then put another spot on top of the first.
3 Repeat several times, making sure the spot does not get bigger.
4 Put the paper on the beaker.
5 Put a drop of water on to the spot; leave a moment to spread.
6 Put another drop on and leave it to spread. Repeat, not adding drops too quickly.
7 Watch the colours separate.

Blob pictures

You will need:

> Non-absorbent paper
> Poster paint
> A paint brush

1 Fold a square of paper like this.
2 Unfold paper. Put it this way up.
3 Put blob of paint right in the middle.
4 Lift up the four corners and bring them together (with the help of a friend).
5 Put it down flat and push the paint outwards.
6 Open out. Dry out and repeat with a smaller amount of a second colour.

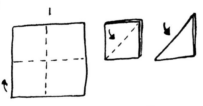

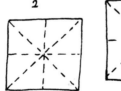

SHADOW PUPPET

Uses: with stories that have an action theme, (eg lame people being healed.)

Make a simple shadow puppet by following template and fastening limbs with paper fasteners. Attach 5 thin sticks such as plant support canes to the limbs and use the sticks to manipulate the puppet. You will need a bright light and a blank wall or screen. Put the puppet between the light source and the screen (or make a puppet theatre from a large cardboard box, with the opening covered in a white piece of translucent material).

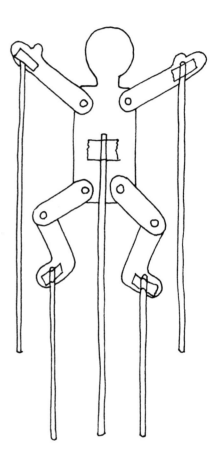

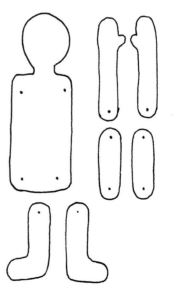

WEAVING

Young children enjoy weaving and creating patterns using different colours – but they often get in a tangle (literally) and need sorting out. The simple cardboard loom (see illustration) will give good results.

1 Make a cardboard loom from a piece of card about 9 x 14 cm. Snip cardboard at top and bottom as shown. Tie end of wool to top corner (a) and wind on the warp.
2 Weave weft (with sticky tape wrapped around one end) under and over the warp.

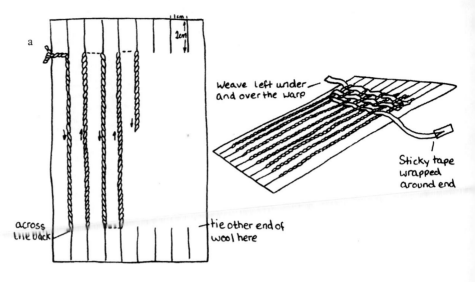

ROSETTE

These simply-made rosettes can be used to decorate cards, party hats or even as badges.

1 Cut two different coloured strips of crepe paper – both approx 30cm long but one about 13cm wide, and the other about 9cm wide. Lay the narrow strip on top and pleat both strips together.
2 Bind together tightly with pipe cleaner.
3 Open out into a circle and staple ends together at back to secure.

'DON'T FORGET' NOTECLIP

Uses: *this activity can be used to make small gifts, eg for Mothering Sunday or other occasions, or when the topic is about remembering, as in God's promise to Noah, or the story of the ten lepers healed by Jesus.*

You will need:
   1 wooden clothes peg
   1 piece of cardboard (approximately 11x5cm)
1 Write the word 'Remember' in the centre of the card and colour in a decorative border (or decorate as wished with stickers, felt tip pens, flowers cut from paper or magazines, etc).
2 Paste the card to the peg.

18 Templates

In this section you will find a number of useful templates which can be adapted for different activities. By photocopying, enlarging or reducing them, you can use them for such diverse activities as making puppets of all kinds, (see lolly stick butterfly puppets in **God's world**), stencils, pictures, mobiles, cards ... and anything else you can think of.

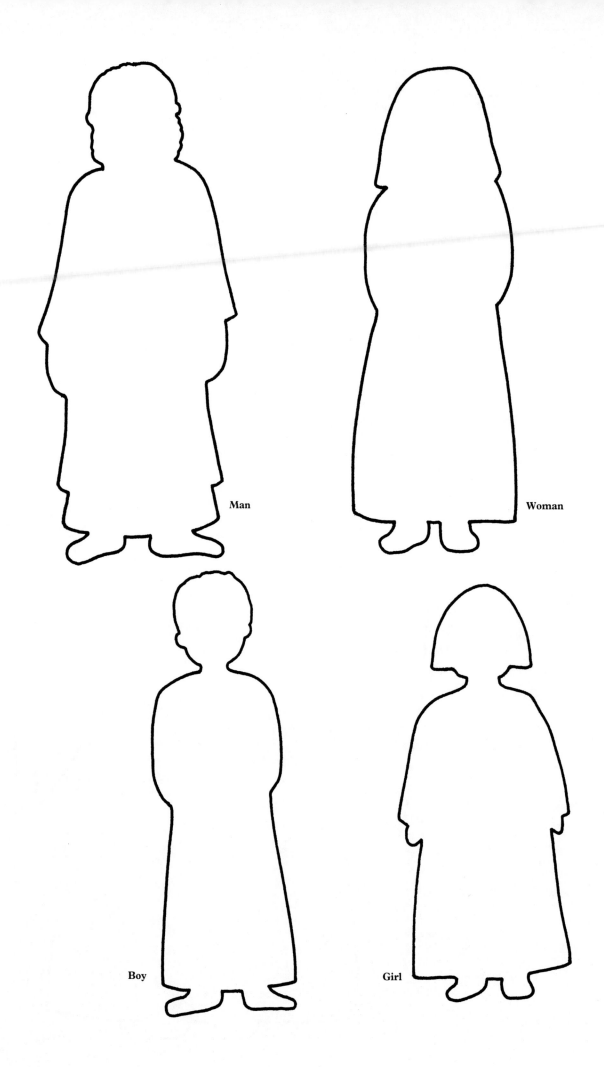

Man

Woman

Boy

Girl

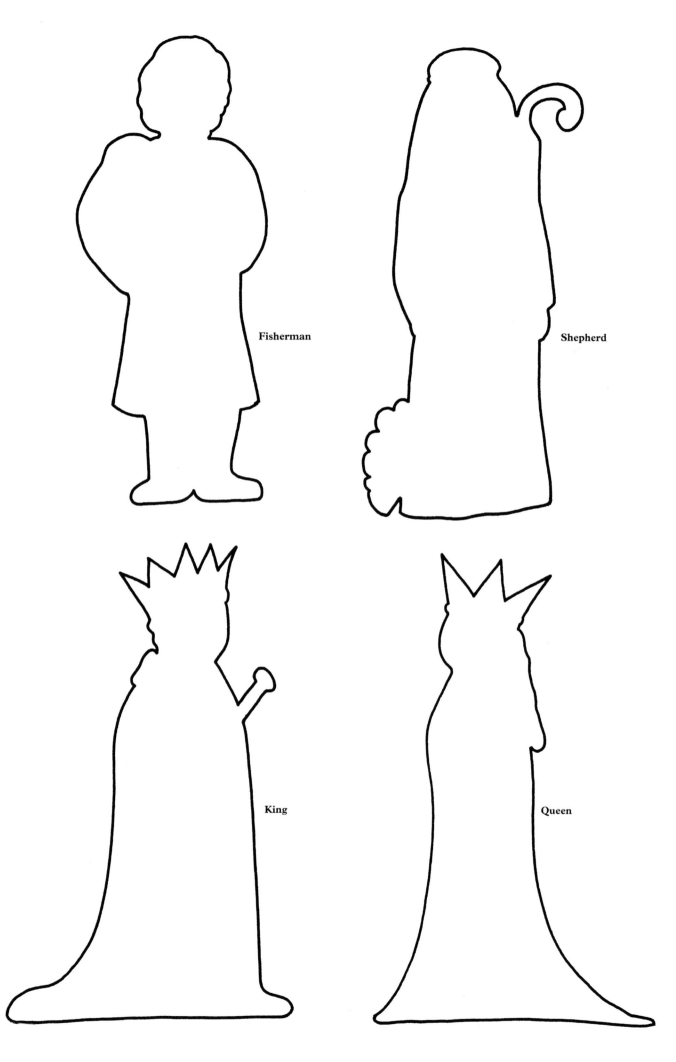

Fisherman

Shepherd

King

Queen

91

Soldier

Soldier

Prophet

Priest

Index